A WORSHIPPER'S GUIDE
TO

CREATIVITY,
SONG WRITING,
AND
MINISTRY

DENNIS JERNIGAN

Our purpose at Shepherd's Heart Music Publishing is to:

•Lead hurting, wounded people to health and life through faith in Jesus Christ
•Lead people into a deeper understanding of their identity through faith in Jesus Christ
•Lead people to freedom from the bondage of sin
•To make Christ known

A Worshipper's Guide to Creativity, Song Writing, and Ministry
©2005 by Dennis Jernigan
All rights reserved. Printed in the United States of America.
Published by Shepherd's Heart Music, Inc.,
3201 North 74th Street West, Muskogee, Oklahoma 74401

Shepherd's Heart

1-800-877-0406

www.dennisjernigan.com

ISBN 0-9765563-0-8

Edited by Teresa Burgess
Art design, Israel Jernigan
Front Cover and Interior Photography, Hannah Jernigan
Back Cover Photo, Josh Reeder, www.joshreeder.com

Scripture quotations marked KJV are from The Holy Bible, Authorized King James Version. Scripture quotations not otherwise marked are from the Holy Bible, New International Version®. Copyright © 1973, 1978, 1984 by International Bible Society. Used by permission of Zondervan. Scripture quotations marked "The Message" are from The Message. Copyright © 1993, 1994, 1995, 1996, 2000, 2001, 2002. Used by permission of NavPress Publishing Group. All rights reserved. Scripture quotations marked NLB are from the New Living Bible. Copyright © 2003. Used by permission of Tyndale House Publishers.

Contents

Dedicated to

*Melinda - for
loving me so completely*

*Israel, Anne, Hannah, Glory, Judah, Galen, Raina,
Asa, and Ezra - for the way you inspire me to love*

*Annie Herring - for teaching
me to be a song receiver and for singing over me*

Matt Vandiver - for always believing for the best

*Jonathan Firey, Ryan Redding, and Caleb Jernigan - for allowing
me the honor and privilege of speaking into your life - for
helping inspire this book*

*Stephen Hinkle - for
being the first one God allowed me to mentor in worship*

Kathy Law - for fighting for me and with me

Kevin Perry - for being a friend and brother

*Tom Hopkins - for being an example of grace in the
midst of unbearable circumstances - you inspire me*

*New Community Church - for being home - for being a
place to practice what I preach*

Dennis Disney - for seeing that 'different' may be best

Mom & Dad - for being there...no matter what

Robin & Trish - for your servant hearts

Foreword

The principles contained in this book are by no means the be all and end all of worship, creativity, or ministry. The things I share in these writings are simply some of the basics of ministry I have learned since November 7, 1981. If you desire to be the best minister to others you can be, this book is for you. If you desire to be more creative in any field, this book is for you. If you desire to be a better song writer, this book is for you. If you desire to know how to be a better planner and to know how to bring major projects to completion, this book is for you. If you desire to know how to do big things for God with the minimal resources you have, this book is for you. Take the principles I discuss and apply them to your life and particular talents.

Why a book discussing worship, creativity, song writing, and ministry? Had it not been for God's intervention in my life during a time of worship I can honestly say I would not be here today. Because the prison walls of my life were blown down due to the sensitivity, creativity, and song writing ministry of someone else, I was led to freedom. When someone finds freedom, gratitude is the result. This book is an expression of my gratitude...and is my way of helping others understand the endless possibilities available to those who are willing to submit their gifts to the Lord...regardless of whether they are musical or not!

God seeks the hearts of men. A broken heart can spill forth His glory and reach to others in need. The place of freedom in ministry comes only from an intimate relationship with Jesus Christ. Above everything else, I urge you to never seek a ministry. Simply seek Jesus Christ with all your heart. Ministry will naturally flow out of this relationship. People in need will seek you out. You will never lack for ministry.

Dennis Jernigan

> *"...seek first his kingdom and his righteousness, and all these things will be given to you as well." Matthew 6:33 (NIV)*

SING OVER ME

My Story

My Story

I am often asked, "How do I get started in the music ministry? I feel God has gifted me and called me to share in a public ministry." I remember having this same question 19 years ago. The only problem I had was in finding anyone who could really give me a definitive answer. The best way I can explain the things I have come to know is to share with you a brief history of my own journey.

Having been raised on a farm far from the influences of any major cities, I was surprised to find that such a thing as 'contemporary Christian music' existed. I didn't realize there had been a 'Jesus' movement or that many 'modern' songs had been birthed as a result until I went away to college. Needless to say, I was so excited to hear all these wonderful melodies that said what my heart had longed to say through music for many years. Being a church music major, I quickly decided (as did most of my contemporaries) that this must be God's calling for my life - not because God had spoken this to my heart but because this was one more way for me to be accepted - one more way to bolster my low self-esteem. The only problem with this was that no matter how well I performed, I was still left with an empty feeling inside until my next 'fix' - my next performance.

In 1978, I had the privilege of hearing and seeing Keith Green live. He was not like anyone I had heard up to that point. He seemed to be more than a musician. In fact, it was as if the music was only an extension of His heart and that his life had gone to a depth I couldn't comprehend or hope to attain to at that time in my life. I know that God had set me up. How could I want to continue the pursuit of a music ministry when I had come face to face with the holiness of Almighty God. Keith scared me...but I liked the way my heart felt after listening to one of his songs. I know now that this was simply the presence of the Lord - and that entertainment was not on the Holy Spirit's agenda for my life.

A year later, I was introduced to the ministry of The Second Chapter of Acts. Because I was privately dealing (not dealing, really) with homosexuality, rejection had a deep stronghold on my life. But as I listened to the words and music from the heart of Annie Herring and her siblings, I would find rest and peace and a hope I needed to carry me through the next three years of my life. Again, as with Keith Green, I was challenged to look at my own heart. But even more than that, I was being wooed by the Holy Spirit to give up to Jesus. He was calling me to wake up and realize He was deeply concerned and intimately acquainted with every area of my life.

At this time in history, Keith Green and The Second Chapter of Acts were the 'top' artists on the contemporary music scene. In fact, they were making waves because of some of the stands they were taking - like not charging admission to their concerts; like having a heart tender towards the needs of the particular groups of people they were sharing with; like Keith giving away his albums for 'whatever you can afford.' The reason I share these things is because in their lives I saw something different in their ministries - and I wanted to be like them. A standard had been raised up in my life and I wanted to live up to it.

Upon my graduation from OBU in 1981, God began to move in supernatural ways that even I couldn't see! One of these instances was a concert by The Second Chapter of Acts in Norman, Oklahoma. At this time in my life, I was struggling with the sin of homosexuality (that's another story) and was looking for anybody who was real - someone who had a real walk with the Lord. And among Christian musicians, I was looking for more than entertainers. So, I went to their concert. I knew by the words they said and the music they sang that these people were genuine, and the message was born out of times of desperation in their own lives. I needed hope. As I listened to Annie Herring speak and sing, I was overwhelmed by the love she spoke of. This was the love I had dreamed of but still couldn't believe was available to me! So I listened very intently with great expectation - until she came to the song "MansionBuilder." This song caught my deepest attention because of the simple phrase, "Why should I worry? Why should I fret? I've got a MansionBuilder Who ain't through with me yet!" All of a sudden she just stopped in the middle of the song and said, "There are those of you here who are dealing with things that you have never told anyone and you are carrying those burdens and that's wrong - that's sin and you need to let those hurts go and give them to the Lord. We are going to sing the song again and I want you to lift your hands to the Lord - and all of those burdens that you are carrying, I want you to place them in your hands and lift your hurts to Him." This was all new to me - worship and praise. I had always thought before that this was just an emotional response that didn't really mean anything. But you know what it did for me? As I lifted my hands, God became more real to me than I had ever imagined! The lifting of my hands was more than a physical action. My hands were an extension of my heart! I realized that Jesus had lifted His hands for me - upon the cross. I realized that He truly was with me and He truly was beside me and that He was willing to walk with me and carry me and just be honest with me. And I could be honest with Him! At that moment, I cried out to God and lifted those burdens to the Lord and said, "Lord Jesus, I can't change me or the mess I've gotten myself into - but you can!" And you know what? He did change me!

At that time I acknowledged the fact that I was a totally helpless and I turned everything in my life over to Jesus - my thoughts, my emotions, my physical body...and my past. Basically, I took responsibility for my own sins and yielded every right to Jesus - my right to be loved, my right even to life. Because of my choice to sin, I deserved death and hell - and that's where Jesus came in. At that point, something wonderful began to take place in my life...I began to hear the Lord speak to my heart - "Dennis, I love you. Dennis, you are my child - I love you no matter what. Dennis, I will always love you!" It was then that I lost the need to be accepted or loved by others because I realized Jesus would love me and accept me no matter what, even when I was rejected by others! It was also at this same time that those sexually perverse thoughts and desires were changed...and He began to replace them with holy and pure thoughts about who I really am.

Soon after this life-changing experience, God led me to realize it was through the principles and instruction of God's Word that I would be able to see that my self-worth could never be realized in my performance...and that people didn't need my performance anyway. People needed to hear God's heart as spoken through the canvass of my life message. Both Keith Green and The Second Chapter of Acts had been birthed into ministry by the Holy Spirit. Because of the healing and deliverance and restoration God had brought into their lives, He saw fit to bless His body with their messages of hope and challenges to a deeper and more intimate relationship with the Holy Spirit. This was to be one of the most profound and life-changing truths in my life.

One year after that concert I found myself teaching school - something I said I would never do! (The year before I had spent as a school bus driver! How's that for credentials in the contemporary music arena?). God was trying to teach me that He desired that I deepen my message in Him - get to know Him. Since God had changed me, I just desired to minister! By this time He was giving me many songs. He had used that year as a bus driver to teach me to cry out with my heart to Him. By 1983 I was married and by 1986 had 2 children with 1 on the way! In 1985 God led Melinda (my wife) and me to a church in Oklahoma City. It was here that God confirmed the truth to my heart that He would broaden my ministry as I sought to deepen my message - deepen my relationship with Him. From 1985 on I purposed to never seek ministry...that I would just seek Jesus. The practical way this worked was this: from 1981 I had asked churches and groups for opportunities to minister to them. But I wanted to know that it was God bringing the ministry. So, I stopped asking and began waiting on God. If He truly wanted me to share somewhere then He was going to have to make them call me!

In 1986, God did a miraculous work in my life personally and in the life of the body we were a part of at that time. Melinda and I had been at the church for approximately 1 year. At that time, a most godly man had been the minister of music and worship leader for 14 years. But one Sunday morning as we prayed before the service, God spoke to him that he was standing in someone else's place and that Dennis Jernigan was to be leading the worship. At that time, our pastor told us that God had spoken this very vision to Him six months previously and that he was to say nothing - that God himself would make a way. (He had spoken this to his wife when God had spoken it to him just to verify that God had done it!). That very morning I led worship for the first time! And the character of Christ was displayed through the life of the former worship leader as he stayed and became the church administrator! It was also at this time that God began giving me songs for our body.

In July of 1988, God called me to begin sharing my story of God's redemption and restoration in my life with others. As I shared my 'story,' people began to have hope in their own situations. As I shared, many gained healing from past wounds or failures and freedom from besetting sins! As I shared, God honored us with His sweet presence and His joy filled our hearts. Although I was told that sharing my past would ruin my ministry, it had just the opposite affect. What Satan had meant for evil God was now using for good. What had been the greatest failure of my life God had redeemed and was now using to minister life and hope to others. It was then that I realized that music is not my ministry. People are! Music became the tool for sharing my heart and an avenue to lead others to do the same!

As God began to spread the word of my testimony to others, a desire for the music God gave me began to spring up as well. Instead of going the usual route of signing with a major company (and I have had many opportunities now), God called me to allow Him to do it His way! As the demand for my music grew, I simply made it available. Our first recording was made by putting up two microphones during a couple of worship services and recording the whole album on a four-track cassette recorder! The sheet music was produced in lead sheet form on our own Macintosh computer! Thus, Shepherd's Heart Music was born! I am so grateful to God for all He has done. I can truly say it is His hand that has moved in my life and ministry. Who would have thought God would redeem a boy from the country who was bound up in homosexuality, give him a wife and family, place him in a small inner-city church, and then give him a ministry that is literally reaching around the world? Certainly not me! I can honestly say that He is a much better 'orchestrator' of my life than me! And I can also say that He has done it - and I tell you all this to boast in the strength and goodness of my Lord Jesus Christ!

So, has God called you to the ministry of music? Or has He

called you to deepen your message and allow Him to broaden your ministry? Has God called you to perform and entertain or has He called you to lead others into an ever deepening intimacy with Him through the Holy Spirit in an atmosphere of worship? Your situation or circumstances may be different than mine but our solution is the same. Seek Jesus and not a 'ministry.' Don't seek your fulfillment through performance. Serve people by meeting their needs. Lay down your life, your reputation, and your definition of success and see what God will do! The next chapter contains some truths from God's Word that have really been helpful to me. Listen with your heart and see if they might not be of help to you as well.

GETTING STARTED
GOD HAS CALLED ME...
NOW WHAT?

Getting Started

God has called us all to go. We are all called to minister! Jesus said, "...You shall be My witnesses both in Jerusalem, and in all Judea and Samaria, and even to the remotest part of the earth." (Acts 1:8) He also said, "Go therefore and make disciples of all nations, baptizing them in the name of the Father and the Son and the Holy Spirit..." (Matt. 28:19) My life verse is Psalm 107:1-2, which says, "Oh give thanks to the Lord, for He is good; For His lovingkindness is everlasting. Let the redeemed of the Lord say so, Whom He has redeemed from the hand of the adversary." If we, as the redeemed, don't say so, how is the world around us which is in dire need of redemption ever going to know there is a way out of their mess?

> Deepen your life message and allow God to broaden your ministry. Jesus said, "...*Seek first His kingdom and His righteousness; and all these things shall be added to you. Therefore do not be anxious for tomorrow; for tomorrow will care for itself. Each day has enough trouble of its own.*" *(Matt. 6:33)*

Intimacy with God is of the utmost importance. Intimacy means I turn to God and say, "Lord, 'into-me-see'" and understanding that He says to us, "Child, 'into-Me-see'." Ministering to the needs of people goes hand in hand with this truth. How can we meet the needs of people unless we come to know them in an intimate way? And how can we get to know people in true intimacy if we don't know the Father in an intimate way? God is concerned with relationship. Jesus said, "And you shall love the Lord your God with all your heart, and with all your soul, and with all your mind, and with all your strength. " But He went on to say, "...You shall love your neighbor as yourself. There is no greater commandment than these." Mark 12:30-31 In John 15, Jesus tells His disciples that our only capacity to 'give life' is if we abide 'in Him.' Our only capacity to love like Jesus is if we have received love from Jesus. In other words, our capacity to love others is directly related to our ability to

11

receive love from the Father. As I have determined that people come first, the opportunities for ministry have not ceased. And more often than not, a song is born out of these ministry opportunities and then goes on to minister to others. It is very difficult for me to write a song just to write a song. For me there has to be a purpose. And the only purpose that has any validity for me is in how it will minister to the needs of people - and not whether it follows all the rules for writing a 'hit' song!

Skill yourself to minister to the needs of people.

> *"Take my yoke upon you and learn from Me, for I am gentle and humble in heart, and you will find rest for your souls."*　　　　　*Matthew 11:29 (NIV)*

A man or woman may be incredibly gifted musically and lack a true depth of character. True Christlike character is directly related to the level of intimacy we have with our Father. Spending time with Him one tends to become like Him! Yes, I daily practice my skills - not to be a better showman or entertainer but to better communicate God's heart for and to His people. More important than being musically skilled is to be 'spiritually' skilled to minister. This kind of 'skilling' takes time just as does musical training. Time must be spent getting our own hurts healed. Time must be spent one on one with individuals. We may plant seeds in large gatherings but just where does true ministry take place? If we follow Jesus' example, true ministry takes place when we spend time with those to whom we are ministering - on an intimate level. Again, most of my songs are born out of my relationships - whether with God or with others. The following Scriptures can be applied to both our musical/ physical training and our spiritual training. Get some 'hands on' experience. Invite some hurting soul over tonight and pour your life into theirs - and then keep doing it. Soon, others will see the life in you and want it. For me, this has happened as I share my testimony. Others hear and want to be free. How can I help in just one sitting? I take those God calls me to minister to personally 'under my wings' and find help for those I can't personally minister to. What has happened is that God has helped me grow in sensitivity to the needs of others and how to best meet their needs - how to get to the roots of their problems. Proverbs 18:16 says, "A man's gift makes room for him, and brings him before great men." This is a principle of God's Word. But how much more meaningful and eternal when a man's gift is given over to the leadership and strength of the Holy Spirit! Another way to look at it is found in Proverbs 22:29 which says, "Do you see a man skilled in his work? He will stand before kings; He will not stand before obscure men." What greater honor is there than to skill ourselves for the service of the one true King and to stand before Him? I can think of none! Intimacy with God is the bottom line. When this is our heart and attitude, we will be flooded with more ministry than we can handle. Getting to know someone - getting to know God and His heart takes time...which leads me to my next point.

Take Time To Prepare.
> *"He who is faithful in a very little thing is faithful also in much..."*   *Luke 16:10a*

Jesus served His parents until He was 30 years old. This was not wasted time. He was God and was already prepared to minister just because of Who He was. The time He spent, though, was valuable in the development and release of His character. We know that God's Word tells us that Jesus grew in wisdom and stature (Luke 2:52). Joseph, Moses, John the Baptist, Paul the apostle, and the disciples all spent years in preparation. Jesus often took time out to get away for refreshment and preparation. Yet, these individuals really were ministering by being faithful in the small things until the time of their public release. Your heart is a vessel made for pouring out the character of Christ and the character of Christ is essential to a fruit-bearing ministry.

A Servant's Heart is the heart of a true minister.
> Jesus said, *"...The Son of Man has come to seek and*

13

Is that what we have been called to do? In speaking to His disciples He also said, "...Whoever wishes to become great among you shall be your servant, and whoever wishes to be first among you shall be your slave; just as the Son of Man did not come to be served, but to serve and to give His life a ransom for many." (Matt. 20:26-28) We need to constantly allow the Holy Spirit to search our hearts and cleanse the leaven - the sin - He finds there. Pride has no place in the life of a minister. When we are servants, we are humble and moldable. When we are prideful, we are lifted up and hardened to God's voice - and the fall is not pleasant - and it will surely come! A servant is sensitive to the needs of those around him. A servant finds life in laying down his life for others. A servant does not seek to make a name for himself, but rather, for the one he serves. If you are gifted musically or in the area of leading worship, simply seek to meet needs. Worship privately. Lead your family in worship. Lead your friends in worship. Lead your home church in worship. What better way to serve than to lead those you love into an intimate encounter with the Lord Jesus Christ.

Find someone who is doing what you want to do and learn from them.

> *"...the things which you have heard from me in the presence of many witnesses, these entrust to faithful men, who will be able to teach others also."*
>
> *2 Timothy 2:2*

Just because everyone else is going to college or seminary doesn't mean you have to! One of the best things I ever did was to sit (for several years now!) under the ministry of godly men who were doing the work of ministry - the very thing I desired to do. It was in this apprenticeship relationship that I not only learned the theory of true ministry but was able to see it lived out in the lives of these men. I now have a young man of 17 who regularly does what I do in my place when I am out of town. He not only capably leads our body

14

in corporate worship, but he also has the job of transcribing all of the songbooks from our recordings for publication - and he started when he was 16! How has he learned? By simply observing what I do and allowing the Holy Spirit to help him glean from my life the things he will need for his life.

God has called us to make disciples. What does that really mean? Not only are we to lead others to Christ but we are to teach them to lead others also. Paul wrote these words to Timothy, "...My son, be strong in the grace that is in Christ Jesus. And the things which you have heard from me in the presence of many witnesses, these entrust to faithful men, who will be able to teach others also." We have much to learn from our elders - from those who have been there. Wisdom is much more important than skill. Wisdom is seeing every aspect of life from God's point of view. Get wisdom!

What about a recording or publishing contract? Wouldn't this get the music out to the most people?

"The mind of a man plans his way, but the Lord directs his steps."   *Proverbs 16:9*

'And [Jesus] said to them, "Why is it that you were looking for me? Did you not know that I must be about My Father's business?"   *Luke 2:49 (NIV)*

Follow the leadership of the Holy Spirit. Many people have the idea that to gain a recording contract or to sign with a publisher is to have 'made it' in the music 'ministry.' While the Lord may desire to use a publisher or recording company to advance His ministry through you, He may want to do something totally new and fresh with you - unencumbered by the demands of a publishing company. And believe me, there are demands. Why, he may even want to raise you up as the publisher of your own music. That's what happened in my life. As people desired the music God gave me, I simply made it available. As the demand, or the need, grew, the Lord provided the means to expand and make the music available on a larger scale. Don't limit or underestimate the wisdom, power, or creativity of

Almighty God. All I can say is be sure you are in the center of the Lord's will. Money and fame are distractions and must be approached with deep humility and much grace. Personally, I am enjoying seeing God take the music all over the world...without the use of an established distribution company. He is my distributor...and word of mouth, the testimonies of others, has been the best advertisement of the music God has given me. Bottom line, though? The lives of people. We must never get away from investing our life in the lives of others - in a one-on-one setting. Jesus felt this was important. So should we.

Trust the Lord as the Giver of Music - the Giver of Songs.
"The Lord is my strength and my song, and He has become my salvation." Psalm 118:14

I am often asked, "How do you write a song?" My answer may seem quite simple, but I believe it is true. I don't consider myself to be a 'song writer' but more a "Song Receiver." (This will be discussed in more detail in a later chapter). My goal is to put myself in a position to hear God for the songs He would sing to me. Yes, I suppose you would say I am a song writer in the sense that God has given me certain abilities to write both music and verse. The difference in my heart, though, is that I cannot force a song to be birthed. The way in which a song is birthed, while varying in 'labor,' are all born out of the same 'womb.' That womb is my heart. As I deal with certain issues in my own life, as I repent of sin, as I hurt with a hurting brother, as I rejoice with a sister who has been blessed in some way, as I see a spiritual need in someone's life, as I seek God for encouragement, etc. (the list is endless), I believe God has a song for any occasion. I cry out to God with my heart in the form of a song - no matter what the circumstance. My desire is to allow the Holy Spirit to conceive 'life' in me - a song - that in turn will bring life and/or edification to those who hear it. My ministry - our ministry - has to be what Jesus' ministry on earth was (and is). My ministry is people and meeting their needs. As I seek to meet the needs of people songs get birthed. Some labors are short and

16

sweet. Others are long and bitter. Some are relatively easy. Some are horrendously painful. No matter what the labor is like, the new 'life' is always a joy to receive and I soon forget the pain and rejoice in what God has brought forth as a ministry or encouragement to others. I do not choose to write a song just to write a song. I choose to be God's vessel of life to the body of Christ. I long to hear His voice and His songs being sung over me. Since that is what He does for me, I want to do that for others. The only way I can be a "Song Receiver" is to be in an intimate relationship with the Song Giver!

Ps. 32:7   Thou art my hiding place; thou shalt preserve me from trouble; thou shalt compass me about with songs of deliverance. Selah.

Ps. 42:8 Yet the LORD will command his lovingkindness in the daytime, and in the night his song shall be with me, and my prayer unto the God of my life.

Zeph. 3:17   The LORD thy God in the midst of thee is mighty he will save, he will rejoice over thee with joy; he will rest in his love, he will joy over thee with singing.

In receiving songs there are some steps, when allowed to be used by the Holy Spirit, which I have found to be very valuable in receiving songs. I believe there is no end to the songs God wants to give. He is Creator. His creativity is endless. As long as there are people with needs, there will be songs that need to be received and shared. As long as there is a God to worship, there will be songs that need to be received from the Song Giver and given right back to Him in worship. The following are some of the things that have helped me.

Believe God is the Song Giver and that you are His vessel - the receiver.

Ps. 40:3 And he hath put a new song in my mouth, even praise unto our God: many shall see it, and fear, and shall trust in the LORD.

As a new creation in Christ, we are caled into relationship with Almighty God. Relationship requires both giving and receiving. I have found the best givers are also the best receivers. The best receivers are also the best givers. When life is exchanged between the new creation and the Creator, life is always the result! Believe this and receive the abundance He has for you.

Skill yourself to write down what you hear.

Pr. 22:29 Do you see a man skilled in his work? He will stand before kings; He will not stand before obscure men.

If you were to tell me you had a great desire to serve me through the gift of writing letters and asked me to tell you the most important of messages I needed delivered to my family, it would make sense that you be able to write down accurately the things I would speak to you, right? But what if I were to tell you that I had a very important message that I needed for you to write down and take to my family yet you didn't know how to write, I would probably wonder if you really meant what you said or if you were trying to earn my approval or the approval of others. I may even wonder if you value me at all. I believe that God is looking for those who would be willing to learn the skills necessary to write down what they hear. The skills of musical notation and theory are of major importance. If you lack these skills, God may raise up another to write down what you hear (even a tape recorder is better than nothing!) or show you some other creative alternative. But even these other means of notation aren't always available. But because I took the time to learn basic music theory and notation, I am ready to write down what I hear - even if no manuscript paper is available. I have used napkins, notebook paper, and even grocery sacks to notate songs I have heard. God doesn't always speak just in my quiet or alone times with Him. God can use you at the level of ability you are at presently. My desire is to be an ever growing 'receptor' of all He has for me.

Be ready to hear from Him at all times - at the drop of a hat!
Ps. 45:1 My heart is inditing a good matter: I speak of the things which I have made touching the king: my tongue is the pen of a ready writer.

I have no idea when the Lord may choose to sovereignly 'drop' a song into my heart. I just don't want to miss Him! I have been awakened in the middle of the night. I have been 'pulled over' to the side of the road. I have been in the midst of a group of people. I have been on the back of a horse. I have been skiing down a mountain. I have been flying at 40,000 feet. God chooses the most wonderful and often humorous times to speak to His children. I want to be ready. I keep a manuscript book and pen with me most of the time. If those aren't available, I get creative. Those are the napkin, grocery sack, or envelope times (billing envelopes are great)! I also have a mini-cassette recorder that fits in my brief case. I write down anything I hear at a later time. Be ready at all times!

Spend time alone with God - sing your prayers to Him.
Ps. 104:33 I will sing unto the LORD as long as I live: I will sing praise to my God while I have my being.

As I have already said, an intimate relationship with the Holy Spirit is vital if you are going to have a music ministry. Because God sings over me, I often have the opportunity to sing over others. This always brings so much healing. In my own life, I have realized that to sustain my life - my true life - I, the branch, must be connected to the Vine - Jesus - or death will surely come. For this reason, I am very jealous of my times with the Lord.

19

See Your Home as a Worship Center.
"For where two or three of you are gathered together
in My name, there I am in their midst." Matt. 18:20

I remember the first few times I led in a worship setting. For me it was in the garage of the family that took me in. We only knew a few songs, but we sang them in sincerity to the Lord and longed together for God's presence. I played and worshiped. They simply followed me. And nothing had changed! My home (the same home by the way!) is now a place where people can come and worship with me. I see my main function as a 'worship leader' is to discern the feelings and needs of the people I am leading and then to discern the will of the Father as how to best lead them to have an intimate encounter with Him. I simply cry out to God on their behalf and for myself and trust the Holy Spirit to woo them to Himself. You must see yourself as a shepherd. A good shepherd discerns the needs of His sheep then leads them to green pastures for nourishment or beside still waters for a drink or rest or into the fold for protection or the binding of any wounds or to hold a frightened little lamb....I think you get the picture! Never beat your sheep. Trust the Good Shepherd, Jesus Christ, to do the work.

So Do You Really Want To Minister Through Music?
"Do not forsake her [wisdom], and she will guard
you; Love her and she will watch over you."
Proverbs 4:6

"Watch over your heart with all diligence, for from it
flow the springs of life." Proverbs 4:23

Wisdom is simply seeing every situation and circumstance in life from God's point of view! And the bottom line really is relationship...with Jesus and with others. I can personally have more impact on one person over a long period of time than I can on a group of thousands I lead into God's presence one time. Yes, seeds may be planted...but I want to give God the best possible return for

His investment in my life! If I can invest my life in just one person a year, and then they in turn invest their life in just one person per year (and so on and so forth!), then my impact for Christ will be much greater than any other way. This was the example we have in Jesus. The best thing God ever showed me was the best thing I can tell you: You simply work on deepening your relationship with Him...and let Him broaden your message or send you out.

I pray that you would take all I have written before the Lord and see if He would give you any insight into your own life through what He has done in mine.

SMALL BEGINNINGS
...TWO FISH...
...FIVE LOAVES...

Don't Despise Small Beginnings

When I graduated from college, I was academically prepared for the world of church music - traditional church music. You know, three hymns, offertory, a special song before the sermon and that was it. Times were changing, though. The world was becoming a much more me-centered place than ever before. Our culture was leading people down a road of self-centeredness like it has never known. Slowly but surely, the enemy was making great headway into our very being as a nation. The homosexual agenda, though always present, was now being pushed more and more to the forefront. Traditional marriage was being attacked like never before, teen pregnancy rates were growing year after year. All we had called sacred seemed to be under attack.

I had always assumed that I would get a job on some church staff and begin rising through the ranks of my denomination to ever bigger and better music programs. The only problem was that the very thought of this tended to make me sick. Why? Because that very form of ministry - traditional church music ministry - had not met any of my needs...especially when I was in the very throes of my own struggle with homosexuality. I needed something real. I wanted something more tangible than I had experienced before. As you already know from my story, God had different plans for me and my life - and a very different way of ministering to others.

Since honesty about my own sin and redemption seemed to minister to others, I simply began doing more of that...in any way I could. If honesty had been the first step towards my own freedom, perhaps my honesty would serve as a catalyst for transformation in the lives of others. I just knew there were other hurting people out there who needed what I had found in an intimate relationship with Christ...but there were no songs that truly reflected the cry of a wounded, hurting heart. As I sought God for songs to sing over the needs of those I was in relationship with, He was faithful to meet me daily and give songs for very specific situations. We would sing these new songs together and needs would be met. Soon, others began asking God for the music...and Shepherd's Heart Music was born!

23

I share these things with you in order to show you that God is more than willing to pour Himself out upon those who are prepared to seek Him...to those who are willing to listen (in those early days, I heard the Lord tell me He would give me a song a day if I would listen...and I still believe that). God can use amazingly small and feeble resources to do amazing things if we trust Him. In fact, it is when we are faithful with and in the small and feeble beginnings that He desires to place greater responsibilities and ministry opportunities upon our shoulders. Are you in a small church with very little resources, tools, or gifted people but have a great passion and vision for the type of ministry I am talking about? Here's my story. I think you'll be encouraged.

My first real worship leading position was not in a church. As the Lord was directing my path toward November 7, 1981, I found myself driving a school bus for a living shortly after graduating from college (how's that for a hopeful beginning?). Two dear friends and I would gather weekly around an old piano in a friend's garage and seek God in worship. We were three dumb kids from traditional church backgrounds who knew there must be more to God and to knowing and experiencing Him than we had experienced to date. We would sing and worship for hours. We only knew a few worship choruses...but this is significant for several reasons. This was where I really began leading others in worship while seated at the piano. This was the time when God began to pour songs into my heart as I cried out to Him (I had applied to the Theory and Composition Department in the OBU School of Music and had been told there were no openings because any open positions were being held for students who had displayed potential for writing on this level...I was crushed). This was where I began to learn to be honest about my feelings and to honestly express them to God in worship.

During this same period - 1982 - one of my heroes went to be with the Lord. I remember the time and place vividly when I heard about the plane crash. I was heartbroken. I felt such an upheaval in my own spirit. Keith meant so much to so many young musicians like me. What would we do now? Who would lead us now? Even though I had never met Keith, he was still a mentor from afar. I wanted to play the piano like him. I wanted to minister like him. I wanted to write and record like him. Lord, I will take his place! Even as I thought those thoughts toward the Lord I heard His reply.

> "I don't need another Keith Green. I have one already. I need a Dennis Jernigan."

This moment was to have a very profound impact upon my life and view of ministry. I had been set free less than a year before, but with this episode I began a new phase of discovering my identity and destiny in Christ.

Do not despise these small
beginnings, for the Lord rejoices
to see the work begin...
Zech. 4:10 NLB

You already know the story of how I came to be a worship leader on staff at a church. I did not know how to lead people. I did not know how to organize a music ministry with real ministry at its heart. I wanted to avoid the very appearance of performance but still wanted to make a place for all the gifted people God was bringing our way. Many of the things I desired to do were simply impossible to do because we had no money. This was to be a very creative time in my life. Lack of money forces one to look at their hopes and dreams from brand new perspectives...and that is what I began to do.

Don't despise small beginnings...

I had seen the most beautiful banners declaring the names of God in other church sanctuaries, but when I priced the materials I found we were lacking. It was upon this news that my pastor's mother told me about some butcher paper that was stored in the church basement. She asked me if I thought there was any way we could make our banners using this? I knew this was God's best for us in this situation. I bought a couple of cans of metallic paint in gold and silver. I bought some cheap latticework slats and built 4'X8' frames for a set of banners of 8 covenant names of God. I simply calligraphied the name 'Jehovah' with the translation 'I Am' under each 4'X8' banner. From these, we hung 14' banners lengthwise. On these long banners were names like 'Shammah' with the translation 'Present' or 'Shalom' with the meaning 'Peace'. In the shape of a 't', these banners hung around our auditorium from the high ceilings. Bringing an air of majesty and reverence to the room, we soon had people calling and coming by to take pictures of our beautiful banners. Many were shocked to learn they were not made of velvet and gold and silver lame'!

Don't despise small beginnings...

As a worship leader for a church body, I felt it was my place to act as a shepherd for my sheep. If there was a need, I wanted to minister to it in a musical sense. If there was a spiritual direction God was taking our body, I wanted to be there with the music. God began to give music, but there was still no way to share that music except during regular worship services. I began to make 'piano-top' recordings with my cassette recorder. If someone was in the hospital and God gave a song, I was there with a tape. If I could not make a tape, I was there with my guitar. It soon became apparent that many desired recorded versions of the songs God was giving...but once again, I had no money! What to do?

By 1986 I had saved enough money to buy a Tascam 4 track cassette recorder! I believe it cost me around $400.00 - a lot of money for a man with several children and a miniscule budget to work with. Even though I had no clue as to what I was doing, I rigged a microphone to face the congregation and placed on on the piano. I then recorded a worship time and played a pitiful little drum line in after the fact on my remaining track. Voila! I had my first real worship recording. We affectionately called the recording 'Dennis and the Crows' because another worship leader had told me they liked the songs but the singers sounded like a bunch of crows! I didn't care...and obviously people didn't either. The first two years after we released that cassette we sold or gave away over 60,000 copies!

Don't despise small beginnings...

Out of necessity, my own publishing (self-publishing) company was born in 1988. After many days of agonizing over a name, my wife Melinda suggested we call it 'Shepherd's Heart Music' because she felt this name best described my heart and vision...and I knew instantly she was right. As of this writing, that was 17 years ago. Now I get to minister with people like Dr. James Dobson and Beth Moore. I get to lead worship with men like Charlie Hall and Joel Engle and Chris Tomlin. I get to travel all over the country and tell my story of God's redemption and watch people get set free. I get to hear my music sung in countless foreign tongues and hear reports from literally thousands each year all God is doing through the music and message. Who would have thought this could ever be possible for a guy from a small country town who grew up to drive a school bus - who struggled with homosexuality - who was told he had no potential to write music? Certainly not I. But isn't that just like God? He takes the fish and bread of our lives and transforms these 'small offerings' into amazing things by virtue of His amazing love and grace. Our little becomes much in His mighty hands.

Don't despise small beginnings...

Did I ever feel like giving up? A lot. Did I ever get depressed? A lot. Did all my dreams come true? No. But what has happened is that I have learned to entrust God with the little (or much) I have been given. I have learned (and still learning) to respond with His love and grace to the circumstances of my life. I simply take what I learn and then use that knowledge to more effectively minister to others around me...whether in my living room or in front to thousands

I have tried to learn to meet the needs of people. In meeting needs, I am simply doing what Jesus did when He walked the earth. My main ministry is not a recording or a great worship event in which thousands attend. My main ministry is not on a church staff or in

27

some book I write. My ministry is to whoever I happen to be with at any given moment. My ministry is in my living room with the couple whose marriage is falling apart. My ministry is in the hot tub with the minister who has been voted out of his church. My ministry is on horseback with a man who feels no joy or purpose in his life. My ministry is driving down the road with a friend who needs to be encouraged. My ministry is to my wife and to my children. My ministry is to my friends. Public ministry is simply icing on the cake for me...and that is the truth. You want to minister? Learn to meet the needs of people.

What do people need? Just look around you. Look at your own life. What do you need? What does your family or your friends need? People need good news. They need hope in the midst of affliction and grace for the fiery trials. They need comfort for broken hearts and they need their wounds bound up. People need freedom from bondage. They need to see beauty from the ashes of broken and burned out lives. People need someone to fill the voids of the heart. They need joy. They need cleansing from sin. You, as a worship leader...or more rightly...as a believer and follower of Jesus Christ can help meet those needs with the resources you have right now. Trust me. You will never know, though, if you always have some excuse for stepping out. Remember the parable of the talents found in Matthew 25:14-30. You have been given something to invest in God's kingdom. Do something with it...now. Use it or lose it.

> *Now it is required that those who have been given a trust must prove faithful.*   *1Cor. 4:2*

> *"Whoever can be trusted with very little can also be trusted with much, and whoever is dishonest with very little will also be dishonest with much.*
>   *Luke 16:10*

So what would keep us from using what He has given us?

Pride

But he gives us more grace. That is why Scripture says:

> *"God opposes the proud but gives grace to the humble."*   *James 4:6*

> *Humble yourselves before the Lord, and he will lift you up.*   *James 4:10*

Fear

> *For God did not give us a spirit of timidity, but a spirit of power, of love and of self-discipline.*
> *2 Tim. 1:7*

> *For you did not receive a spirit that makes you a slave again to fear, but you received the Spirit of sonship. And by him we cry, "Abba, Father."*
> *Rom. 8:15*

Weariness

> *Let us not become weary in doing good, for at the proper time we will reap a harvest if we do not give up.*   *Gal. 6:9*

> *"Come to me, all you who are weary and burdened, and I will give you rest. Take my yoke upon you and learn from me, for I am gentle and humble in heart, and you will find rest for your souls. For my yoke is easy and my burden is light."*
> *Matt. 11:28-30*

WHAT IS WORSHIP?
INTO-ME-SEE...

What is Worship?

Having been raised in a non-charismatic church, I had no idea there was any difference between worship and praise. Having now had the opportunity to worship with my charismatic brothers and sisters, I realize they do not either! Before anyone gets the wrong idea, I am a spirit-filled believer. I desire to be a part of the body of Christ and not to be separated by petty differences. Jesus Christ is Lord. Period. The last 20 years of my life have been spent pursuing God in a way I never dreamed I would. I came to the point where I was tired of the 'death' and 'dryness' of my religious traditions. When I plunged into the charismatic world, I became disillusioned at the 'flakiness' and lack of character I saw. What I soon realized is that I still wore the grave-clothes of both worlds. Inside I was dry and dying. Inside I was wishy-washy and in need of Godly character - the fruit of the Spirit. It was upon my own recognition of these short-comings that I set out on a most incredible journey - to know God for myself. What I soon came to understand was that the deepest needs of my heart would be met in one way...that the answers to all my questions would be found through one means...that the only way to know God in the deep way I desired would become reality by one thing: RELATIONSHIP!

In the presidential election of 1996, the Clinton campaign kept one word in the forefront of their election team's mind: It's the economy. By keeping their focus, they were able to fend off the distractions of the opposition and to keep their heads together as a team, thereby spinning even the worst of issues to their favor by always changing the subject back to the economy. For me, relationship is the word God has spoken to my heart. I knew Jesus was Lord. I confessed with my mouth as much. I believed He was the Son of God and that He had risen from the dead. I knew all the right things to say and do. I just didn't know that relationship was required...much less what it really meant.

Relationship, in its simplest form, means 'to be connected or to enjoy kinship.' To me, relationship is a two way street. I receive the life of Christ and I give back to Him and He receives from me!

31

What a concept. No one had ever told me this was possible...at least not to the degree I have come to realize in my own life! Throughout the course of this book you will read that one word over and over - relationship! To know about God or to know He knows me is not enough. To have some type of interchange is where the rubber meets the road. A lack of relationship in the life of a believer can be pictured like this: The Sea of Galilee is full of life and freshness. It receives the rain and runoff from the surrounding hills and, in turn, nourishes the plant and animal life within its banks as well as the farmland of the surrounding area. The water within its confines flows out of the Sea of Galilee and into the Jordan River. The Jordan River is also full of life and sustenance as it winds its way to the Dead Sea. The Dead Sea, in turn, receives all the same life-giving water yet it is dead! Why? Not to over-simplify, but the reality is that the Dead Sea is dead because, even though it receives 'life', it gives nothing back. In other words, the relationship between the two bodies of water is a one way street. As believers, we are called to live in relationship with Jesus Christ. He is real and alive and desires an intimate and ever-deepening relationship with each one of us. After all, didn't Jesus say He would give us life...and that life more abundantly? Now that we have a picture of what this book is about, let us begin to define some very essential elements of how that relationship is to be developed.

What is praise?

When I first set out on my journey to know God (way back in 1981!), I had just graduated from college with a degree in Church Music. Needless to say, the only job I could get at that time was that of a school bus driver. What I soon realized is that God had engineered all this to put me in a position to begin getting to know Him. Since I didn't even know where to begin, I simply sat at the piano each day between my morning route and my afternoon route and sang my heart out to Father. At first, all I knew to do was to place my Bible on the piano, opened to the Psalms of David and cry out David's words in song to Jesus. What I found myself doing, more often than not, was simply thanking God for all He had done in my life. As I look back on those times I now understand that what I was doing was simply taking my first baby steps. Much as a toddler who is first learning to walk towards the outstretched arms of his Daddy, I was doing nothing less than the same toward my heavenly Father! The truth is this: I had simply begun to praise Him through the expression of gratitude. What I found was spiritual legs on which I no longer had to crawl but could now walk - and, yes - run toward the Father with.

So, what exactly is praise? Most dictionaries give definitions of 'admiration, appreciation, or commendation.' I like the way Webster defines it: 'admiration or gratitude expressed'. Gratitude or gratefulness is simply 'being appreciative of the benefits one has received'. As I sang through the Psalms day after day, I discovered that whenever words of praise were used by David, they were almost always in the context of gratitude, extolling the ways in which God had benefited his life. In other words, praise is simply 'giving thanks to God for Who He is and for what He has done'! Psalm 107:1-2 (two of my 'life' verses) reads:

> *"O give thanks unto the Lord, for He is good: for His mercy endureth forever. Let the redeemed of the Lord say so, whom He hath redeemed from the hand of the enemy;"*

Another aspect of praise is simply declaring or telling others what God has done:

> *"Come and hear, all ye that fear God, and I will declare what He hath done for my soul."*
> *Psalm 66:16*

Having been set free from the sin of homosexuality in 1981, gratitude was heavily on my mind. I readily had an affinity with Paul, 'the chief of all sinners', when he said:

> *"And I thank Jesus Christ our Lord, who hath enabled*

33

me, for that He hath counted me faithful, putting me
into the ministry; who was before a blasphemer, and
a persecutor, and injurious: but I obtained mercy..."
1 Timothy 1:12-13

Gratitude expressed becomes praise. Praise becomes a springboard into the deeper places of relationship with Almighty God. Gratitude should be the attitude of every worshiper. Yet, the simple truth is that even a non-believer can express gratitude to God for something He has done. One can believe in God yet not know Him. In other words, praise does not necessarily require relationship. I have seen people, void of a life-changing relationship with God, receive something (like healing or financial needs met) and readily thank God for what He had done...only to go right back to the ungodly life they had lived prior to God's intervention. We have all seen movies in which the 'hero' is lost at sea or in some dire situation. At some point he makes the statement, "God, if you get me out of this, I'll change my ways." Of course, the hero always make it and 'thanks' God verbally, but nothing else changes. Did he praise God? Yes. Did he have a relationship with Him? In both cases, I would say he did not. One can praise God and not know Him. But I believe one cannot worship God without a true knowledge of Him - without a 'knowing' relationship.

What is worship?
Quite literally, the word 'worship' means 'to acknowledge the worth of something. But what does that really mean? How does one find the true worth of something unless he gets to know that one? And how does one get to know the Creator of the universe in such an intimate way? I personally believe that worship is living out my relationship with God through Jesus Christ by the power of the Holy Spirit. Proverbs 3:5-6 says:

"Trust in the Lord with all thine heart; and lean
not unto thine own understanding. In all thy ways
acknowledge Him, and He shall direct thy paths."

34

In other words, if I will seek to know Him in, with, and through every area or aspect of my life, He will direct my paths. He wants to be intimately involved in my life! I had always thought God was a cosmic policeman whose only interest in me came whenever I messed up. Upon the occasion of my sinning, He would zoom into my life, zap me with some punishment, then zoom out again to resume His distant and controlling stance over me (much like the church-police or Pharisees of our day!). What I have since come to see is that He is not distant at all, but is as near as I will allow Him to be. Not only that, but He speaks to me as I speak to Him. I sing to Him. He sings to me. I dance before Him. He dances with me. I bow. He cleanses. I fall. He picks up. I sin. He redeems. I seek to know who I am. He gives me my identity. Do you get the picture? There is way more to God than we have ever realized...or ever will.

If worship is simply living out my relationship with Father, how do I 'flesh' that relationship out? In simplest terms, worship is obedience to God. Obedience requires surrender of our wills to the truth of His will. Giving up 'my' will is not some loss of personal identity as we see in the practice of many cults. Obedience and our subsequent surrender means understanding that I desperately need God - even more than I need the air I breathe. The true reality is that I need Him to hold me to this earth, not gravity. Who made the gravity? Who made the air I breathe? Who gave me life in the first place? Who overcame homosexuality (that I could not overcome myself. I tried!) and bore it on the cross for me? I can do none of those things for myself. I certainly could not save myself. Only One could do that. Jesus Christ. The truth is that I need Him to meet every need of my life...and ultimately, He does!

Do you know God to the depths that you desire? Do you think you know all you need to know of Him? I admit, there are days when I find it difficult to hear God and to know Him in an intimate way. But isn't the recognition and confession of that need the first step in a relationship? Communication. Worship is communion with God! Communion requires expression. Love not expressed is not love. Paul was faced with the same reality when he wrote to the church in Corinth. He confessed he did not know God as fully as he desired.

And he even confessed he could only see God dimly at times:

> *"For now we see through a glass, darkly; but then face to face: now I know in part; but then shall I know even as also I am known."*
>
> *1 Corinthians 13:12*

Worship is presenting our hearts to God and saying, "Lord, here I am. I cannot see You for the dust of this life has settled on the glass of my heart and I can only faintly see You. Would You please take me to Yourself and wipe off that dust so that I might see You and know You a little better?" Worship is trusting God enough to let Him take your heart and cleanse it - free it - of anything that separates you from Him.

Why do we worship or praise God?

God's Word does command us to praise Him and to worship Him. Yet, God does not force us to love Him. The beauty of any relationship that bears fruit and life is that it is entered into of and by one's own choice. God chose me, and He allows me the freedom to choose Him in return. Yet, because of the holiness of God, we know that one day every knee will bow and every tongue will confess that He is Lord. That is reality simply because He is God. The beauty and awesomeness of our God is that He still never forces us to love Him. So why do we have verses which command us to love and worship Him? I believe it is because He provided the law (His commandments) to be like teachers which guide us to the truth. Ultimately, we need God and we need to know Him. Like a parent who commands his/her children to do their homework because he/she knows that child will need that 'knowledge' to succeed in corporate life at some point, Father blessed us with His law because He knew we would need to know Him if we were to truly succeed at life! He commanded us:

> *"And thou shalt love the Lord thy God with all thine heart, and with all thy soul, and with all thy mind."*
>
> *Deuteronomy 6:5 (See also Mark 12:30)*

God is Creator. We are the creation. The creation always reflects the heart of the one that created it! If He loved us, then isn't our heart's deepest desire to love Him? Isn't the heartcry of all mankind to know God? I believe if everyone were honest, they would have to say that there is an emptiness - a void - deep inside that compels them to know their purpose for existence. For the believer, that purpose is more easily seen. Again, we see why the law is needed: to guide the unbeliever to see his or her need for something to fill that void...for something greater than themselves! All that was created by God was created to bring Him glory - to reveal that 'createdness' that is who we are. The only way to fully know and live in that reality is to come to grips and terms with a relationship with the Creator of all that is.

> *"For by Him were all things created, that are in heaven, and that are in earth, visible and invisible, whether they be thrones, or dominions, or principalities, or powers: all things were created by Him, and for Him: and He is before all things, and by Him all things consist."*   Colossians 1:16-17

> *"Thou art worthy, O Lord, to receive glory and honor and power: for thou hast created all things, and for Thy pleasure they are and were created."*
> *Revelation 4:11*

> *"For we are His workmanship, created in Christ Jesus unto good works, which God hath before ordained that we should walk in them."*
> *Ephesians 2:10*

Worship is an act of confession. Our outward life is merely a reflection of our inward life - who we really are (or at least who we think we are!). If we do not outwardly confess Christ, aren't we really denying Him?

> *"Whosoever therefore shall confess Me before men,*

37

him will I confess also before My Father which is in
heaven. But whosoever shall deny Me before men,
him will I also deny before My Father which is in
heaven."   *Matthew 10:32-33*

Another aspect of confession - of relationship - is healing. James 5:16 says:

"Confess your faults (sins) one to another, and pray
one for another, that ye may be healed. The effectual
fervent prayer of a righteous man availeth much."

How does confession bring healing? If I went to a physician seeking healing for a certain ailment but would not tell him where I hurt, how could I be healed. Confession is not for the doctor but for the patient! Yes, God knows where we hurt...but do we trust God (the Great Physician) enough to allow ourselves to be vulnerable enough to be healed? Sin is the ultimate ailment. When the 'cells' of our heart have been rid of the 'germs' of sin by the 'antibiotics' of redeeming blood, life is no longer hampered and the flow of relationship is once again restored...and healing of the soul takes place. Do you see how confession is simply one more aspect or facet of worship? If we desire health in our souls, then, as with our physical bodies, we must feed our souls with the proper diet: a diet of relationship through the food of praise and worship.

"Praise ye the Lord: for it is good to sing praises
unto our God; for it is pleasant: and praise is comely
(becoming)." Psalm 147:1

In other words, praise looks good on you. Praise does a body and soul good! If praise does that, worship - the depth of relationship - will do the same...and more!

What is another facet of worship? When Christ is lifted up, He draws others to Himself (John 12:32). As I have praised God publicly through my testimony of redemption...as I have sought to allow the intimacy I have come to know with my God to permeate my existence...others who have found themselves in like situations have come to seek Jesus because of what they have seen. As I have shared the intimate details of my relationship with Jesus, He has used that knowledge to draw others to see that their deepest needs can be met through knowing Him just as mine were.

What does God require of a worshiper?
God simply seeks to know those who will worship Him in spirit and in truth (John 4:23-24). The most simple application of this Scripture is that He desires that whatever I express on the outside (the truth) should be a result of whatever is on the inside (the spirit). People will hear my words but will look at my life to see if there really is power or life in what I say (Ezekiel 33:31-32). God Himself looks at the heart (1 Samuel 16:7). Shouldn't that tell us something about the truth of what it means to be a worshiper? Like a glass, here is my heart...and I see You rather dimly, but You see clear within me, cleansing every trace of the dust I've let build up that keeps me from what I love dearly...to see Your face more clearly...I just need Your love and grace...'til I see You face to face.

Face to face with Almighty God. That really is the
deepest desire of every person. Some face that day
with dread and fear, others with hope and longing.

Worship is communion or back and forth communication with God. God sees us - even the things we hide - and He still loves us. God desires that we have an honest and open relationship with Him. But to know God is to realize that we can not know Him without being changed. Change is good - because His change brings us closer to the reality of who we really were created to be - more like Him, our Father. As with healing, honesty requires confession. Confession requires trust. Trust paves the way for relationship. Relationship is the conduit - the vessel - of life. God just wants us to be honest.

"We refuse to wear masks and play games. We don't
maneuver and manipulate behind the scenes. And we
don't twist God's Word to suit ourselves. Rather, we

keep everything we do and say out in the open, the whole truth on display, so that those who want to can see and judge for themselves in the presence of God." 2 Corinthians 4:2 (The Message)

God desires that we be either hot or cold. This is simply another aspect of transparency or honesty with God (Revelation 3:15-22). God desires a grateful heart expressed to Him and to others. Gratitude is like a spring-board into the depths of the pool of God's heart (Colossians 3:17). A worshiper must worship out of love for the Father and out of genuine love for those he leads or desires to reach. Otherwise, his/her love is simply so much noise. (1 Corinthians 13)

Why do we need to worship in an outward way?

As I earlier stated, love not expressed is not love (John 3:16)! What is expression but the outward manifestation of or communication of something that we know or feel or experience on the inside? If I never told my wife I loved her or never demonstrated that love to her in some tangible way, would she know I loved her? My thoughts may be totally consumed with love for her but she would never experience those thoughts as relationship if I never shared or demonstrated them! Jesus demonstrated His love by dying for us! I have had someone say to me something like this: "What if you were deaf and blind and could not move your physical body? How can you say that love not expressed is not love to someone who cannot express it?" If I were that person described, I would use whatever means I had available to me to express my gratitude and love for God. If all I could do was blink an eye or think a thought, that is what I would do! But that is no excuse for those of us who can freely move and say and do! We were given bodies with which to express. We were given emotions with which to express. We were given voices with which to express. On and on and on! God has made a way for us to express our relationship to Him and, in turn, receive relationship from Him through our physical members! My spirit and soul when coupled with the 'apparatus' of my body becomes a powerful tool of relationship with Almighty God this world needs to

40

see and know and experience for themselves. God knows our heart, but the act of expression is important for life to take place. Worship is an act of communication and an expression of relationship.

Questions for meditation:

•What masks am I wearing to present myself to others in a dishonest way?

•What games am I playing to try to protect myself and hide my pain or weaknesses from others?

•Do I truly express my love for God in a tangible, life-giving way?

•Do people see me as superficial or sincere? What steps can I take to put off the insincerity and put on the truth?

•What would keep me from worshiping God in spirit and in truth?

•What is prayer...but talking to or communing with God? How can this truth be made more real in my life with Him?

How to Minister
What are their needs? What do YOU feel towards them, Father?

How to Minister

As a worship leader, I have come to expect the Lord to use me to minister to the hearts of His children. Of course, God is to be worshiped first and foremost, but worship requires that we focus on Him. For the person who just fought with his wife on the way to the service or to the mom who is distracted by the worry of whether her sick child will recover, this is not always the easiest task to perform. For the man whose business is failing to the man whose family is falling apart before his eyes, focusing on God may seem impossible when faced with the overwhelming nature of our very real circumstances. How do we lead hurting, distracted people to place their focus upon the God who can meet their needs?

David was King of Israel. David was a worship leader. But long before David became King or penned that first Psalm, he was a shepherd. I am sure that one of the first things he was taught as he watched his father and brothers tend to the family flock was how to assess the needs of the sheep. Where do you think Psalm 23 was inspired? A great deal of those powerful, comforting words were directly drawn from David's own experience as he remembered meeting the needs of his own sheep. His sheep were well watered. His sheep were always being led to green pastures. David's sheep were well protected, having David there with his sling and stones to fend off the lions and bears and those who would steal the sheep. David even wrote these words of wisdom to his own son, Solomon:

> *"Be sure you know the condition of your flocks, give careful attention to your herds...." Proverbs 27:23*

Even when I am leading worship for a group of people I have never met before or spent any time with, I ask the Lord to give me a sense of their needs. When I approach times of ministry - whether leading worship for a large group or sitting in my living room with one person in need - I simply ask two questions of the Lord:

1. Father, what are the needs of those in this room? Give me a sense of their needs on every level.

2. Father, what do YOU feel towards them? Let me feel what You feel.

In asking those questions, I have surrendered my own heart to that of the Lord. More often than not, the Enemy tries to get me to focus on my own circumstances as I approach leading worship. Often it is out of my own need that I lead. I have learned that it is not coincidence when I am faced with a particular need. The Lord allows me to go through trying times in order to lead others through the healing process of a right response to difficult situations. In asking those two questions, I refocus my own heart and hear His answers for myself...and more often than not, others have come with similar needs in their own lives. As I come to a sense of His heart (hear His answers to the questions), I then am prepared to proceed accordingly.

This may sound overly simplistic, but it is honestly how I begin to minister. Some may say, "It's not about these people. It's about God," and they are correct. But what is the point of beating people over the head with truth if love is not first extended? Most of the time, people who come to worship God simply carry the baggage of their lives in with them. One of my jobs as a minister is to lead them to lay those burdens down on Someone who can honestly carry the baggage for them. The bottom line really becomes this: Lead people to freedom and they WILL worship! We will discuss these principles of ministry in greater detail in later chapters.

The Healing Aspect of Worship

You Will Know The Truth

The Healing Aspect of Worship

When we lead others in worship, we are literally leading them to an encounter with or an opportunity for intimacy of relationship with Almighty God. To have an intimate relationship with God is to get to know Him - and to allow Him to get to know us. We basically lead people to a place of having the lies of this world confronted with the truth of who God is. This makes the act of worship - even in a corporate setting - a very potentially life-changing encounter every time we have the privilege of leading others. This is one of the greatest responsibilities I know in life. With worship comes a realization of God's presence. With His presence we find His very nature. His nature is one of truth - and truth always has a way of bringing healing.

You will know the truth and the truth will, what? Of course we all readily know the answer. The truth will set us *free* according to John 8:32. What does this have to do with worship and its healing facets? In my case and from my perspective, *everything*. God's Word is the truth. Jesus is called *The Word of God* (Rev. 19:13) and He called Himself *the way the truth and the life* (John 14:6). The importance of this? I do not have a relationship with a book - the Bible. I love the Word of God but I have a relationship with a real, living Savior who is **THE** truth!

What does it mean to *know* the truth? The word used for *know* in this instance is also used in Luke 1:34. When the angel came to Mary and told her she would bring forth a son, her reply was, "Then said Mary unto the angel, How shall this be, seeing I know not a man?" What did Mary mean here? She was saying she had not had an intimate relationship with a man. If that is the same word used in John 8:32, we can make the statement 'You will have an *intimate* relationship with the Truth (Jesus), and the Truth (Jesus) will set you free!'

What is the first step of Truth?

We often find no power in the words of John 8:32 because we never really get to the truth. Why is that? Because the first step of truth or toward truth is always our honesty. 1 John 1:9 says, *'If we confess our sins, he is faithful and just and will forgive us our sins and purify us from all unrighteousness.'* King David, after he committed adultery and murder, made the following honest confession in Psalm 51:3-4, 17. *'For I acknowledge my transgressions: and my sin is ever before me. Against thee, thee only, have I sinned, and done this evil in thy sight: The sacrifices of God are a broken spirit: a broken and a contrite heart, O God, thou wilt not despise.'* Healing came to his repentant honest heart...because truth always leads to freedom.

In my own life I discovered that honesty is a part of brokenness - and brokenness leads to a place of healing. I would not have been healed of homosexuality had I not gotten honest that it was a problem. I had to agree with God that it was sin...that He had dealt with it through Jesus...that I was already forgiven...and that He wanted to give me a brand new identity. When I became honest, the walls of this particular bondage began to fall away from my heart and mind. The greatest fear I had was of being exposed...yet it was the very act of self-exposure that the Lord honored in my life. My greatest fear became my greatest blessing!

Truth leads to honesty. Honesty leads to intimacy. Intimacy leads to health and life. Intimacy simply means I turn to my Father and say to Him 'Lord, into-me-see' and at the same time, realize His heart is turned toward me and He is saying, 'Son, into-Me-see'. Once I took that first step toward truth, healing instantly began to flood through my soul. This all happened for me in the context of a worship experience.

How do we get the sheep to the place of honesty? As a shepherd, I must walk there first. In other words, when I prepare to lead worship, I must be willing to honestly confess my need for God to those I lead. I never share the details of my sin because details can lead to fantasizing and vain imaginations. I have learned that if I share the attitude that led me to sin, others can feel at ease to confess the same attitudes. When we deal honestly with our own attitudes, others we lead - because we really are like sheep in a good way - are inclined to examine their own lives and follow in our footsteps. This can all be done through the songs we select, the words we use to express our hearts, and our very real moments of crying out to God in corporate settings. In that sense, we really are not worship leaders. We then become *Lead Worshippers*.

Because God so graciously ministers life to me through worship, I tend to use what ministers ot me to minister to others. I have watched people who have been bound up in homosexuality for decades suddenly fall on their faces in repentance during times of worship as they realize God's intense love and mercy upon their lives. I have watched in amazement as men and women contemplating suicide confessed their great need and found hope to go on with life while being bathed in God's presence during a time of worship. I have heard the loud praises of men who were once bound up in bitterness now rejoicing because they not only found God's forgiveness during a time of worship but began to extend that same forgiveness to others - all in the context of worship.

Lead people to freedom and they will worship. Lead people in worship and healing will result. We must be willing to walk in honesty and to lead in honesty, no longer willing to play the religious games of wearing masks and performing for the approval of others. We must find the place of rest God offers each of us through finding our identity in Him. Even if you don't know how to lead someone out of a particular sin pattern like homosexuality, you can still lead them to freedom. How do I know? Because you already know the answer. The answer to any sin problem or identity issue is Jesus! Simply be willing to lead people toward Jesus and you will find God has given you the ability to help people overcome even the most challenging of habitual sin patterns.

Being a minister of healing through worship simply requires your own sincere honesty before God. Honesty leads to truth. Truth leads to freedom. Freedom leads to abundant life. Honesty is not a sign of weakness. I have found quite the contrary...like perhaps in my weakness He is strong (now where have I heard that before?). Being honest is not always easy. We must be willing to receive God's grace to do so. And He offers His grace to us freely and readily. To be effective as a worship leader who truly desires to minister freedom to His flock, we must be willing to be honest with ourselves, with our God, and with those we lead.

How to Maintain a Flow in Worship

Where You lead me I will follow...

How To Maintain a Flow in Worship

What does the phrase, 'flow in worship', mean? Quite simply, when leading others in a corporate or group worship session where songs of praise and worship are lifted to the Lord or where a group is being led to acknowledge the presence of God and to ultimately deal with God's presence, the flow of worship is the way in which each facet or phase of that worship session interpolates with the next. If I could sum up what it takes to maintain a flow in worship, I would have to simply say, *"Be filled with the Holy Spirit."(Ephesians 5: 18-21).*

Being raised in a non-charismatic church left me with a bad taste in my mouth concerning the 'filling of the Holy Spirit.' Yet I knew I had the need of His power in my life. Having grown up without a clear knowledge of all it means to be filled with the Spirit, I was curious. I knew that my life was powerless and that I needed the Holy Spirit to fill me. I knew that. But after spending time with my charismatic brethren, I knew there were just as many excesses and misconceptions about the Holy Spirit in their lives as I had come to experience of dryness in the non-charismatic side of things. Needless to say, I began a personal quest toward being filled with the Holy Spirit - and purposed to not be swayed by either my traditions or by the traditions of the charismatic church.

To give the definitive narrative on what it means to be filled with the Holy Spirit is not my intent here. My desire is to put my personal experience into simple terms in the hopes that my experience will somehow shed light on you and your experience in such a way that we all come to the realization that none of us has all the answers! I fully realize my need for the charismatic side of the body of Christ...and I fully realize they need me! The bottom line? We all need Jesus!

To me, if one is truly filled with the Holy Spirit, there will be evidence. I am not speaking of the 'evidence of speaking in tongues'. Quite frankly, I have met and prayed with many believers who spoke in tongues but had a great deficiency of character. I believe that if I am filled with the Spirit, I will bear forth the fruit of the Spirit! In other words, if I am full of God's Spirit, love, joy, peace, patience, gentleness, goodness, faith, meekness, and temperance will flow out of my life (Galatians 5:22-23).

When I first began asking the Lord to fill me with the Holy Spirit, I expected to speak in tongues...because that is what others had told me to expect. What I experienced, though, was something far deeper and greater than a mere unintelligible utterance. I experienced what I call 'the embrace of God.' I remember feeling consumed with His presence, like I was surrounded so completely below and above that I could no longer tell where I ended and the Lord began...like a ship sinking into God's presence, my heart was flooded - every room, deck, nook, and cranny being filled up to the fullest extent of the depths of God's presence. Not only was my heart consumed, but my heart was changed. The things I had not been able to see in my own life were now suddenly a part of my very being...or at least I could see them. I am talking about the fruits of the Spirit. Where once I could only see myself as despairing and hopeless, I could now see myself as a child of hope and full of joy. Where once I had been full of bitterness and envy, I was now full of forgiveness and encouragement towards others. In other words, I was full of the Holy Spirit. I came to realize that the power of the Holy Spirit that comes with the filling of the Holy Spirit always brings the power to change me. I can not encounter the Holy Spirit without being changed!

By the way, I do believe that speaking in tongues is a valid gift of the Holy Spirit. But it is just that - a gift. Not everyone receives the same gifts. And we do not determine what gifts the Father decides to give nor do we determine when He gives that gift. I just want us all to remember that each experiences the Lord in different ways. The sure test of the gifting and power of the Holy Spirit can be found by simply looking for the fruit. If change has taken place and God has received glory, the Holy Spirit has been there. We really, as new creations, can not leave God's presence. Psalm 139 tells us that if we go to the highest mountain or to the lowest part of the sea, He is there. The problem is simply in our perception. Do we really want to acknowledge the Lord's presence? Do we really want to be consumed by His presence?

In light of what I personally believe about the filling of the Holy Spirit, I simply ask the Lord a series of questions that help me discern my response as a worship leader. I begin by asking the Lord to embrace me and immerse me with and in His presence. I then ask the Lord to speak to me and to give me 'ears to hear' Him. By faith I simply believe that I have been filled - and I never rely on a feeling. Faith supersedes and overrules any feelings I may have. Now having said that, I must put on the balance of that truth and say that it is God who created feelings. I can trust His feelings. To discern what Father is feeling, I ask two questions before I ever begin leading out or when preparing to lead others into an awareness of His presence. Number one: Lord, what are the needs of Your children in this gathering? Number two: Lord, what are you feeling towards Your children? By asking those two questions, I can quickly tap into His heart and follow the leadership of the Holy Spirit as I seek to flow in worship. Feelings become like a thermometer, a gift to help us gauge needs, when we seek to know God's feelings toward us.

I never worry about missing God anymore. Why? Because I have decided beforehand what I will do if I miss God's direction for a particular service or if I misunderstand His feelings or the leading of His Spirit. I simply have determined to be honest with those I lead. If I make a mistake, I admit it, seek forgiveness, and lead on. The best thing a leader can do to lead is to be prepared to humble himself, cry out to God, then go on (Micah 7:8). Remember who you are.

Still and quiet your soul. (Psalm 131)

If I am to lead out in peace, I must come to the place of peace to begin with...become like a child. A child is trusting and desires to be like his Father. A child enjoys pleasing His Father and being with his Father. As a child of God, I must simply follow in faith and confidence of Who He is in me and of who I am in Him. Be who you really are in Christ. (2 Corinthians 4:2)

One of the best things I have ever discovered is that I do not have to be another Keith Green. In other words, I simply need to lead out of who I am. I also stopped trying to perform at a technical level I have not yet achieved. I do set technical goals for myself by leadership

53

of the Holy Spirit. I have learned to sing, play my instrument, and lead out of who I am by practicing my gifting privately. This simply means that all I do on a public scale I have also done while alone with God. I cannot truly expect those I lead to have an honest encounter with God if I have not sought to have one myself.

Carry on a continual dialog between yourself and the Holy Spirit.

Just because I ask the Holy Spirit to fill me before I lead worship does not mean I will have all of Him I need throughout the course of that service. I have learned to ask Him questions in the midst of worship times. Asking a question means I should constantly be listening for His answer. I desire to not go anywhere until I have heard Him. At the same time, I must lead on boldly in what He has told me until He tells me otherwise. In other words, if the last thing I heard Him say was to sing, I will keep singing until I hear Him tell me to stop...in faith.

Trust Him. (Proverbs 3:5-6)

The ministry of worship is to be a ministry of faith. To express my faith in God means I can trust Him to lead me from song to song or from 'place to place'. I can even trust Him to lead me through key changes. Why, I can trust Him to always lead forth in peace. Confusion is not from the Holy Spirit. I need never be afraid to wait on Him or to be silent. Silence used to denote confusion in my life - or fear. Now silence is simply the best and clearest way to hear His voice. Since I lead out in faith, I must think ahead once I have heard His direction. I think through key, tempo, meter, and dynamic changes...all by leadership of the Holy Spirit. At least that is my goal!

Be honest with your people.

If you are part of the body of Christ, you must realize that we cannot allow an 'us and them' mentality when leading worship. We are all in this together, part of the same team...part of the same body but each part having different and needed functions. As a worship leader, you must teach your people that worship is not a performance - it is an act of relationship. Relationships always flourish when honesty is a part of the foundation. Have you ever been part of a service in which a musician or singer makes a mistake and suddenly tries to fix it to no avail? Me, too! It does no one any good to try to blame someone else for one's own mistake or blunder. When you have a 'train-wreck,' don't try to cover it up. Just lead forth in a transparent attitude. Don't make excuses. Just be honest and go on. Your people will feel valued and esteem you for your honesty and humility. After all, a leader leads by example...and God will, from time to time, make an example of your life whether you like it or not! Above all, teach your worship team to be flexible in following you. They, too, receive great blessing and benefit from your humble example of transparency.

Some Practical Steps to Leading Worship

•The leadership must lead out in active worship. Our goal is not to worship simply to experience God. He is worthy of our praise whether we experience Him or not. Our focus should not be on what we do or do not experience, but should rather be on simply exalting God as God! Then, guess what? We will experience Him!

•All worship should have a Scriptural basis and be carried out in faith. Our number one priority should be to make Christ known (Proverbs 3:5-6). Relationship!

•Teach people (congregation) that they, too, are praise leaders. The congregation is the choir!

•Encourage parents to train up their own children in the area of worship and music. Lessons can be obtained!

•Encourage apprenticeship (I Chronicles 25:6-8). If someone in your body desires to learn to read music or to play an instrument or to lead worship, etc., encourage them to find someone they know whom they could spend time with. The best way to learn a craft is to spend time with those who are 'masters.'

•Don't be afraid to learn an instrument yourself, worship

leader! You can flow much easier when you accompany yourself. While this is not mandatory, it is Scriptural. David accompanied himself.

•Don't limit your congregation (or yourself) to simple songs or voice ranges. Encourage them that they are new creations created in the image of God. Teach your people who they are in Christ and that they can skill themselves musically (I can do all things...Philippians 4:13). To lead your people to greater depths of technical prowess does not necessarily even require that they know what is going on. A good shepherd determines the needs and capabilities of his sheep and then leads accordingly.

•Use pictures (analogies) to teach. Jesus used pictures extensively. Why? Because a picture which portrays a spiritual concept is not easily forgotten...because it will be forever associated and easily recalled by simply thinking about that picture!

•See yourself as a brush the Holy Spirit would like to use to paint a picture of Christ's heart before the people.

•See yourself as an artist painting that picture yourself by the leadership of the Holy Spirit. The palette of the riches of His kingdom are at your disposal.

•Teach people how to meditate. Meditation goes beyond memorization. One can mediate or think about one word and ask the Holy Spirit to teach you every angle or

facet of God's character as it pertains to that one word. The possibilities are endless as to all God can teach us through meditation. As a result, our relationship with God is enhanced far beyond what we ever thought possible!

•Explain the form of the song you want to teach. This sets the people at ease because they know what to expect. They can trust someone who doesn't always lead them on a wild goose chase in worship! Teach a new song by section. Tell the people what to expect.

•Ask questions of the worshipers in the midst of a song and let the people answer musically.

•Teach the people to be instruments of worship. Encourage them to allow the Spirit to 'strum' their heart strings. He is the breath of God. Allow Him to 'blow' upon your heart as a flute or trumpet, etc..

•Teach the people that His laws are written upon their hearts. No truths are too difficult for them because their very nature has been renewed and joined with the nature of the God of the Universe (Romans 2:15)!

•Spend time with other worship leaders and learn from one another.

•Encourage the people to worship at home.

•Ask God for songs just for your body.

Planning for corporate times of worship

•Plan by leadership of the Holy Spirit.

•Ask the Lord to give you a sense of what the needs of this particular group might be.

•Ask the Lord to allow you to feel what He feels towards this group.

•Enter your rehearsals with this same attitude and express your impressions to the worship team and choir.

•Spend time in prayer with your team concerning upcoming services or ministry times.

•View each time of worship as vital in the lives of those you are leading. You never know who will be attending or how deep the needs are going to be. Do not take what you do as a worship leader lightly. See each worship time as a potentially lifechanging event in the lives of those you lead.

•Know the heart of church leadership and don't be afraid to share your own visions.

•Be flexible!

•Don't sing the latest songs just because they are 'hits'. Sing the songs that will lead the people in the direction God is leading.

•Find out where the people are and take them where they need to be. Where do they need to be? In God's presence. We simply need to be made aware!

•If the Holy Spirit has given you a list to go by, be sure that each singer, player, overhead technician (flipper), sound technician, etc., has a copy. That list should include song order, keys, key changes, and any other directions you may have from the Lord.

•Have all instruments tuned before people begin gathering.

•Conduct a sound check before people begin gathering.

•Monitors should not be louder than the 'house' speakers. Learn to listen to one another.

•Create an atmosphere the Holy Spirit feels welcome in. He feels welcome in heaven. Find out what is going on in heaven and do that!

•The body needs to be a body, each part fulfilling its function of worship. A worship leader is called to be an exhorter: one who urges another on!

•Set people free to be led by the Holy Spirit - even if they are led to just sit still.

•Don't prod. You are a shepherd. Shepherds lead. You are also a sheep, just like everyone else out there! One sheep must step out and follow the Shepherd. The other sheep will follow a sheep who looks like they know what they are doing...a sheep who seems to genuinely trust the Shepherd, the others follow.

•Introduce new songs as the Spirit leads.

•Teach your people who they are in Christ. Don't limit them or their capability to learn more difficult songs. Look at the songs the children of Israel sang! Psalm 103 was one of their songs (Be realistic, of course!). Exhort the people. Encourage them to have the heart of David when facing Goliath: don't tell me I can't do this!

•Don't force spontaneous songs to the Lord. Lead out but don't force. It's OK for you to sing to the Lord in this manner - even if no one else does! Just use discernment. One man's joy may be another man's distraction. At the same time, distraction can be good...if they are distracted from the traditions of men by the truth of God's love.

•Show deference to people...but greater deference to the Holy Spirit! Just be sensitive to the Holy Spirit.

•Teach players to rely on the Holy Spirit. Encourage them to practice playing from chord symbols and by ear. This may seem impossible to them at first. But 'greater is He that is in me than he who is in the world.' And remember, 'I can do all things through Christ Who gives me strength.'

•Encourage instrumentalists to write their own arrangements. Don't be afraid to give assignments.

•Remind the worship team that they are servants, not stars!

I realize I have thrown quite a lot of little tidbits into this chapter! But I felt they were needed. My prayer is that you will be encouraged to be all God has called you to be...and no more!

HOW
TO
RECEIVE A SONG

YOU ARE MY
ALL IN ALL

How To Receive a Song

People call me a song writer - and that is accurate to a degree. While I do write songs, much more is involved for me than simply being able to craft a song which is good in form. I want to be good at the craft of song writing, but I want to be better at walking in relationship with the Giver of Music. In other words, I don't want the pressure of performance and writing a song people will like to be the motivation for writing a song.

In 1981 I was offered the opportunity to move to Nashville and work as a jingle writer with the added incentive of being able to pitch my songs to artists. As the time came for me to make a decision, the Lord used Keith Green and Annie Herring to cause me to rethink the direction of my life. I had also been offered a job working at a major hotel in Oklahoma City and was told that I could make a huge amount of money on weekends if I would be willing to make myself available for more than just normal busboy duties. I told myself that I needed the money and that I could resist the offers of providing sexual favors. Nashville or major temptation. I needed to hear from the Lord.

Driving to the hotel for my initial interview, I turned on the radio to hear Keith Green singing from Psalm 127: 1 which says, "Unless the LORD builds the house, its builders labor in vain..." I knew the Lord was speaking to me. I knew I could not place myself in a position to be constantly bombarded by temptation. The hotel job was definitely out of the question. As I drove the rest of the way home, having settled that issue, I focused on the need for direction concerning the song writing opportunity in Nashville. Again, the words of the Psalm rang through my head.

"Dennis, are you building the house or am I?" I clearly heard the Lord ask. I knew enough to know that if God would protect me from a major temptation like the hotel job would have been, then He had only my BEST at heart...so I could trust Him enough not to go to Nashville...even though this seemed like the open door I had been waiting for. It was during this period of time that I determined that I would allow the Lord to open the doors of ministry rather than me trying to break them down myself. I knew I would be taking a different path than all those around me. I needed to settle in my own heart that this would be okay in spite of how successful other song writers might be in comparison to what God calls success.

I began to call myself a "song receiver" during this period. Where did I get that idea? God had used the ministry and writing of Annie Herring to change my life. I used to long to write like she did. She seemed to be able to put into words what my heart cried out to say to God. I would hang on every word she wrote or spoke in concert. In several of her songs she referred to herself as a 'receiver' as opposed to being a writer. What did this mean? Pure and simple, to be a "song receiver" means to walk in intimate relationship with God and to write down what you hear Him saying or singing to you. Combining this concept with the rules of good song writing, I began an incredible journey, a journey toward deeper places in my relationship with the Lord, where singing to Him and being sung to BY Him was an integral part of the process...and still is.

Writing in and of itself is a gift...and that is the point. It is a gift from the Creator and was meant to be a tool for relationship and born out of a relationship - and not for the need to be approved of or accepted by others. In other words, I don't have to prove anything to anybody in Nashville. My songs are born out of a real relationship with a real God. To receive means you place yourself in a position to receive. To be a good receiver one must be willing to listen. And a "song receiver" must be skilled to write down what he/she hears or receives.

> *It wasn't so long ago that you were mired in that old stagnant life of sin. You let the world, which doesn't know the first thing about living, tell you how to live. You filled your lungs with polluted unbelief, and then exhaled disobedience. We all did it, all of us doing what we felt like doing, when we felt like doing it, all of us in the same boat. It's a wonder God didn't lose His temper and do away with the whole lot of us. Instead, immense in mercy and with an incredible*

love, he embraced us. He took our sin-dead lives and made us alive in Christ. He did all this on His own, with no help from us! Then He picked us up and set us down in highest heaven in company with Jesus, our Messiah.

Now God has us where He wants us, with all the time in this world and the next to shower grace and kindness upon us in Christ Jesus. Saving is all His idea, and all His work. All we do is trust Him enough to let Him do it. It's God's gift from start to finish! We don't play the major role. If we did we'd probably go around bragging that we'd done the whole thing! No, we neither make nor save ourselves. God does both the making and saving. He creates each of us by Christ Jesus to join Him in the work He does, the good work He has gotten ready for us to do, work we had better be doing.

Ephesians 2:1-10 (The Message)

Writing vs. Receiving

Have you noticed I am differentiating between performance and relationship? I believe there are fantastic writers out there who are gifted of God to write incredible songs. I believe one can write a song that can move hearts in deep ways and never walk in relationship with God. What I have discovered is that God has called me to write songs born out of my walk with Him in order that those songs might reflect His glory and at the same time meet the needs of His children. These types of songs may never make the Top Twenty Countdown, but they might make the difference of life or death in the life of a lost, misguided, wounded, abused soul. It's all about the Lord, but He was about meeting the needs of people. If I can first communicate to the Father what my needs are in a particular situation or what He means to me in the midst of that situation, I can then turn around and share that song with people and watch Him lead them to freedom.

*"Are you tired? Worn out? Burned out on religion?
Come to Me. Get away with Me and you'll recover
your life. I'll show you how to take a real rest. Walk
with Me and work with Me - watch how I do it. Learn
the unforced rhythms of grace. I won't lay anything
heavy or ill-fitting on you. Keep company with Me
and you'll learn to live freely and lightly."*
                    Matthew 11:28-30 (The Message)

Wait a Minute! God Sings Over Us?

That's right! God sings! In fact, I think the only ones gifted with
the ability to sing are people and God. Even in Scripture I can
only find that angels declare or speak the glory of God. Singing is
reserved for the redeemed and for the Redeemer. I first heard Annie
Herring sing a song called 'Sing Over Me' on her last recording with
The 2nd Chapter of Acts in 1988. That set me on a course toward
understanding a little better what it means when God's Word says
in Psalm 42:7 'Deep calls to deep in the roar of your waterfalls; all
your waves and breakers have swept over me.' I began to listen for
Him singing over ME!

Psalm 32:7 says 'You are my hiding place; you will protect me
from trouble and surround me with songs of deliverance.' Who sings
those songs of deliverance? The Lord! In Psalm 43:8 we find the
psalmist saying, 'By day the LORD directs his love, at night his
song is with me — a prayer to the God of my life.' Who gives this
song in the night? It says HIS song is with me! After contemplating
the reality of what this meant for me as a "Song Receiver," I plunged
headlong into the ocean of His love. The God of the Universe sings
over ME!!!!

Why write or receive new songs?

I come from a tradition which says, 'The hymns were good enough
for our forefathers. They are good enough for us.' While I love the
hymns, as I have stated earlier, there just weren't many hymns that
spoke to the bondage of homosexuality! The call from the deeper
places in God's heart to the deepest places in my own was always

64

'higher up and further in.' I had an insatiable desire to hear God for my own needs and to minister to the needs of others according to what I heard Him singing over me.

Beyond that, I simply decided I would obey God rather than men. His Word says from Psalms to Isaiah to Revelation to sing to God a new song! Someone needs to write those songs. Why not me? Colossians 3:16 tells us to sing songs of the spirit. Ephesians 5: 18-19 tells us to make melody in our hearts to the Lord. Like Jesus in Luke 2:49, I wanted to be about my Father's business. From my perspective, His business was singing over me. I would do that for others with the new songs He was birthing in and through my life.

Where do I begin?

Walking in relationship with someone is honestly rather simple. We spend time with them and we ask them questions about themselves and then we, in turn, answer questions that are asked of us. WIth the Lord, it is no different. God desires relationship with us. He loves it when we talk to Him. He loves it when we listen to what He has to say. He simply loves relationship! Here's what I began to do when I realized this.

So many other voices vie for our attention, it is often difficult to hear the voice of the Lord. But we know we CAN hear Him because His Word tells us so. John 10:27 says, 'My sheep listen to my voice; I know them, and they follow me.' We can learn to hear Him. First step? Quiet the other voices. From 1981 until 1993 I did not listen to radio - Christian or secular - or watch TV except for the news. I completely missed the '80s! But in the process, I learned to hear the Lord. I believe He was willing to pour out music on me because I was willing to shut out the other voices in my life.

In the beginning I simply asked Him questions and then waited for the answer. You'd be surprised how well that works!

'Father, do you love me?'
'Yes, son.'
'Father, how much do you love me?'
'I love you this much, son...'

I realize this sounds overly simplistic to you, but that is the reality of where I began to hear the music God sings over all of us. Out of the desperation of my own life and its multiple needs, I learned to listen for God to sing over those needs and the needs of others I was in relationship with. As I heard His voice, I simply wrote down what I heard in poetic form. The sons of Korah wrote this in Psalm 45:1:

> *My heart is indicting a good matter: I speak of the things which I have made touching the king: my tongue is the pen of a ready writer. (KJV)*

> *My heart is stirred by a noble theme as I recite my verses for the king; my tongue is the pen of a skillful writer. (NIV)*

I must skill myself to be the writer/receiver who is ready to listen to and respond to the words of the King. I am ready to receive wherever I am. I have received songs on horseback, on a ski lift, driving down the road, in the hot tub, in the bath tub, during a time of worship, in a church staff meeting, etc. God is more than willing to pour Himself out upon those who are willing to listen!

Where does skill come in? How can you write down what you hear if you don't know how? If you expect others to write out what you may play into a recorder, I believe that is lazy and presumptuous. God gave the song to YOU. Why would you offer back to Him something that cost you nothing? Is knowing God and receiving songs from Him worth your time, expense, and effort? Certainly. If so, are you willing to do what is necessary to skill yourself in this area? Proverbs 22:29 says, 'Do you see a man skilled in his work? He will serve before kings; he will not serve before obscure men.' Many want the glory found in the spotlight that writing and performing can bring but are not willing to pay the price to get there...expecting others to do all the work for them. Be like King David who said in 2 Samuel 24:24, "...I insist on paying you for it [the place to build an altar to the Lord]. I will not sacrifice to the LORD my God burnt offerings that cost me nothing."

Consider your education as you do your salvation - always in process.

Never stop learning. If you want to learn to write music or play the piano or play the guitar, find someone who is doing what you want to do and learn from them. You never know until you ask. You'd be surprised at how often people miss opportunities to learn simply because they would not ask for help. Fear and pride need to be put down by humility and desire to serve God.

I wanted to learn to play the piano like Keith Green. So you know what I did? I bought every Keith Green album and songbook I could find and began to learn by listening! Before I knew it, people were constantly telling me I reminded them of Keith Green! Even today, that is one of the highest compliments I can ever be paid.

If that style of learning will not work for you, find a teacher or go to a good school of music. Pay someone to teach you. I have found that the things I pay for out of my own pocket mean a lot more to me anyway. The lessons become more valuable because my checking account reminds me of the sacrifice I am making to do this. I hold myself accountable to complete my lessons because I don't want to waste my money!

Another option is to buy books on song crafting or basic music theory. You'll be surprised at how quickly you will learn in the process of seeking avenues of wisdom in a particular area of study. You will be surprised at the number of people God will bring across your path as you share your journey/search for knowledge with others. As always, we learn better by DOING. In other words, begin learning and write as you go. The more you practice, the better you will become. I believe God will give me a song a day if I will listen...and He proves Himself by pouring Himself out as I do!

Trust the Lord as the Giver of music - the Giver of songs.

'The LORD is my strength and my song; he has become my salvation.' That's Psalm 118:14. Who is the song? HE is the song! I sing His glory. His love. His redemption. His power. His name. I recognize that the ability to create music was given by THE Creator. If that is true, then I must always put myself in a position

to receive from Him...and you know what that means? I must walk in RELATIONSHIP! If He desires to give me music, I must prepare myself to receive that music by getting in a place to listen!

When I travel, I carry a small digital recorder with me. I also carry manuscript paper with me at all times if possible. The 2004 National Day of Prayer theme song, 'Let Freedom Ring' was first 'written' while driving to see my son at college in Arkansas! I sang it into my recorder as I drove and wrote it down when I got home. I put myself in a position to receive - and God gave! If time is hard to come by, get rid of something to make time. If other factors hinder your ability to receive, then deal with them. Knowing Christ intimately is worth the cost of going without something.

Be creative. What is creativity? Creativity is simply seeing life and circumstances from God's point of view! If you are in a particular circumstance or if you have a friend who faces a crisis, look at that circumstance or crisis from God's perspective and write accordingly...even if it goes against what conventional wisdom calls 'the rules of good song writing.'

Understand that songs are born and that each labor is going to require time and will be different from any previous labor. My wife Melinda and I are the parents of 9 children. No, we are not Mormon or Catholic...just wanted whoever God would give us! When our first son was born, we experienced a lot of uncertainty through the process. By the time our second child, a daughter, was born, we thought we knew everything. Boy, were we surprised when nothing was the same! As in childbirth, pain is involved in the process. Without pain, we would have no clue as to what the needs of the process are. Pain is a sign that attention is required. We discovered in childbirth that pain is best dealt with by learning to work WITH the pain rather than to fight against it. The end result is a beautiful child - or song - that we feel very proud of producing! And each one is certainly worth the pain required!

When seeking God for songs, remember that a servant's heart is the heart we must put on. If we desire to write and receive from God's perspective, we must learn what His perspective is. Matthew 20:26-28 says, *'Whoever wants to become great among you must be your servant, and whoever wants to be first must be your slave — just as the Son of Man did not come to be served, but to serve, and to give his life as a ransom for many.'* Jesus came to serve. We are to serve God and others with our lives and with the gifting and talents He has given us. What did Jesus come to do? According to Luke 19: 10, '...the Son of Man came to seek and to save what was lost.' We are to do the same through the receiving of songs!

Spend time alone with God. (Psalm 104:33)

When first learning how to be a "song receiver," I knew I needed not just quality time with God, but quantity time. As in any relationship, we can say how much more valuable quality is over quantity...but reality says that quality does not come except by quantity. Ask any parent whose children have been wounded by lack of time and you'll find this to be true. So it is with the Lord. Quantity brings quality. During the early days of my 'real life training,' I would spend hours at the piano. Between my morning school bus routes and my afternoon routes I had hours. I would place my Bible on the piano and begin singing from Psalm 1 through Psalm 150. I put into practice what I learned in Psalm 104:33: 'I will sing to the LORD all my life; I will sing praise to my God as long as I live.'

How did this help in learning to be a Song Receiver? I began to see that Psalmists like King David were open and honest with the Lord. If David could be honest with God about his sin (adultery, murder, etc.) and still be considered a 'man after God's own heart' then maybe I could, too! I began to sing my prayers to God and then learned to write them down in song form. These songs became tools of ministry as I began to sing them to others and relate the story of their birth.

If we want to be Song Receivers, we must set aside time for writing/receiving - and then actually use the time for writing and receiving! As followers/disciples of Christ, we must be prepared to hear from Him in our daily living out of our lives, but we must also be willing to carve out time from our busy schedules - even if only 10 minutes - and seek His heart. The more you do this, the more you will receive. During these times of seeking, be prepared to write down or record what you hear.

Develop your relationship with Father.

Matthew 6:33 says, '...*seek first his kingdom and his righteousness, and all these things will be given to you as well.*' Of course, this passage speaks about the way in which God will meet our most basic of needs for food, shelter, and protection. In other words, if God cares about one sparrow which falls to the earth or if He arrays the lily with beauty that reflects His glory, how much more will He do that for His children? Psalm 37:4 tells us to, 'Delight yourself in the LORD and he will give you the desires of your heart.' The word delight means 'to be exquisitely happy' about something. Seeking God in intimacy (which means 'into-me-see') means we allow God to see into the depths of our hearts as He allows us to see into the depths of His! Amazing! If I seek His Kingdom and delight myself in Him, I will have the abundance of all His Kingdom offers me with the added bonus of having the dreams and desires of my heart met. When I seek Him, I know His heart and His desires...and my desires fall into line with His. In other words, I really want what He wants!

One of the best pieces of advice anyone ever gave me was quite simple. Seek Jesus and not a ministry! I want to know Him and to know His heart. Once you know someone on an intimate level, life is exchanged. When life is exchanged, more life is always the result! This is part of what it means to have life and to have it more abundantly (John 10:10). A healthy relationship requires both giving and receiving. What I am discovering is that the best givers are also the best receivers...and the best receivers are also the best givers. It's always about giving but you've got to have something to give...and that comes by being willing to receive. It's actually a very beautiful circle that knows no end. When we learn this about relationship with God, we are then able to transfer this relational process to healthy human relationships as well!

As stated before, song receiving is a process...and so is relationship. Relationship also involves seasons just as there are seasons we must endure in childbirth and in song receiving. There must first be the intimacy - the union. Then comes the conception - the song idea.

70

Next comes the gestation - the growth and meditation. Then comes labor, followed by birth. And then we get to present the new birth - song - to others! Relationship is about life. Seek the Giver of Life and watch what pours out!

Be ready to hear from Him at all times.

I have already said this, but it bears repeating. Just like the Psalmist, we must be ready to write down what we hear...at any time (Psalm 45:1). I keep manuscript paper at my bedside and carry it with me to most places I go. I carry a small digital voice recorder in my car so that I can capture what I hear even while driving down the road. No idea is a bad idea. I write down even little snippets of melodic or lyrical ideas because I know mighty oaks can grow from small seeds! Keep a journal of ideas and remember each song - each birth has its own timetable.

See yourself as a Shepherd. (Psalm 23)

Because I have been involved in local church ministry as a means of keeping my broader ministry grounded in real life, I see myself as a shepherd to my people. As with leading people in worship, I also put on a shepherd's heart when seeking God for music for my people. In leading and receiving in this manner, ask yourself, "Where would a Shepherd lead His sheep? How would He lead His sheep? What are the benefits to the sheep if I lead them to a certain place?" Etc. Be like David in your song receiving.

Lead your people musically to green pastures: spiritual food: the Bread of Life.

Lead them beside quiet waters: quench their thirst with Living Water.

Restore the soul of your flock through song: emotions are important and valid: healing can occur without speaking a word.

71

Lead them to paths of righteousness: to peace: to a better understanding of their true identity in Christ: Jesus is our righteousness.

Through song, lead them to a sense of God's constant presence in their lives.

Lead them to a balance of God's justice and mercy.

Lead them to taste and see that God is good.

Lead them to the feast God has made available to us.

Lead them to put down the enemy by simply following the Shepherd: by exalting Jesus.

Lead them to a place of healing: to reality and balance.

Lead them to the place of gratefulness: an overflowing heart.

Lead them to an understanding of our place in eternity - right now.

Where do I go for inspiration?

There are several places I regularly go for inspiration as a Song Receiver. God's Word is a constant source. Years ago I began practicing meditation. I don't have to memorize massive quantities of Scripture to accomplish this. Meditation can involve one word from a passage. Growing up on a farm, I always watched the cattle or sheep chew their cud - grass they had already eaten which they regurgitate to chew on some more...insuring maximum nutrition is gained from that which was ingested. That's how I meditate on God's Word. I chew on a word like grace, then put it away in my mind. I then bring it up throughout the day for extracting more spiritual nutrients!

The presence of the Holy Spirit in my life is a major source of inspiration. Of course, we know that the very word for Spirit in God's word is the word pneuma which can be translated as 'the breath of God'. God-breathed inspiration. I call these out of the blue encounters. In other words, I give the Spirit permission to intervene in my life at any time. This places my heart in an expectant mode. I expect to be surprised by His presence and inspiration!

Through prayer and honesty comes much inspiration. If I face a difficult circumstance, I cry out to God and sing to Him in honesty. Truth sets us free, but honesty is always the first step of truth. Talking with God in an honest manner often leads to great moments of revelation and inspiration as I get to God's perspective - His heart - concerning the issues of my own life.

In a sense, relationship is everything. Without relationship there is no life. Without life, there is nothing. As with the Lord, relationship with people is vital for inspiration. God placed us here to have relationship. In His body, I have learned to seek His face for those I am in relationship with. As I lift the needs of others to God in prayer/song, I often receive songs that transcend our local body. Having been inspired to receive a song for a specific situation in the life of a friend or family member, I am in relationship which helps others outside my circle latch on to that song for their own situations. Certain themes can transcend local use and often gain a widespread appeal for the depth to which they pierce a heart.

Life circumstances themselves lead us to cry out to God. Of course, I want to cry out to God when things are good, but the natural response of a hurt child is to cry out for their parent. So it is with us. I cry out to God a lot! Even bad circumstances like broken relationships or the physical death of a friend can be used to minister life and to bring God glory.

God sometimes speaks musically to me in dreams. When my friend Kathy needed a theme song for her first comedy album, I woke up with that theme song on my mind! Thank God I had manuscript paper nearby! Often, God speaks to me in the night while I sleep because I have learned to go to sleep meditating on His Word. Psalm 127:2 says that 'He gives to His beloved even in their sleep...' Be inspired as you sleep!

Sometimes, certain situations leave me dumbfounded, lacking words to express the depth of feeling I am experiencing...like the loss of a friend's 6 year old son...his only son. What does one do in these situations? God has given us emotional gifts which transcend spoken words. Even the Holy Spirit practices this. Romans 8:26 says, 'In the same way, the Spirit helps us in our weakness. We do not know what we ought to pray for, but the Spirit himself intercedes for us with groans that words cannot express.' Don't be afraid to utilize the gifts of the Holy Spirit in this manner. Learn to express your heart through tears, groanings, tongues, making melody in your heart, etc.

There are times when words do not come, but my heart is overwhelmed with a need to sing a melody. Inspiration can come as we express in a melodic or musical sense the emotions or impressions that are there in our heart

Most often, I do not listen to Christian music. This sounds terrible but my thoughts are this: I want to hear fresh for myself what God is speaking to me. I do not want to copy what others are doing. At the same time, know that I enjoy hearing what God is doing through the lives of others in the Christian music world. I just limit myself to small portions so I can be assured I am hearing what God wants me to hear. For that reason, I listen to classical music for melodic and harmonic inspiration. I love to listen to modern classical-style music from film scores like Braveheart and Gladiator. I love composers like James Horner and Hans Zimmer. They inspire me to be more melodic in what I do.

Do not be afraid to express deep emotions musically.

When we approach crafting a good song, we often get sidetracked by what is popular at the time. What interests me more is being sensitive to what the Lord is doing at any given time...whether the resulting songs ever sell a million copies or not. A good song is one that evokes a response from the listener on an emotional and on a spiritual level. Emotion expressed in song gives people an opportunity to express more easily what they may have difficulty

74

expressing otherwise. Emotion in song gives people an opportunity to express things they 'always wanted to say' but 'just didn't know how.'

What is emotion? First of all, we must remind ourselves that emotion was created by God. Our God is an emotional God. According to His Word he expresses anger, joy, grief, hatred, and any number of other emotional nuances. Degrees of love are often expressed by depth of emotion. The woman who anointed the feet of Jesus with the expensive oil was making a very emotional statement of how much she loved Jesus...of how grateful she was for His freeing love.

What is emotion? What are emotions? Emotions are the rivers of the soul which carry our deepest feelings to God and act as cleansing agents, carrying the dead waste of our minds to the heart of God and which, in turn, carry and convey His thoughts and feelings back to us in ways we can receive and understand. His emotions bring clean, pure, Living Water back to our hearts. Emotions are a gift from God for expressing our love for and to Him. Emotions are common ground to which all people can readily relate. One of the most powerful emotions - one of the most beneficial emotions of a Song Receiver - is passion. What is passion? The sufferings of Jesus in the period following the Last Supper and including the Crucifixion are often referred to as the Passion of Christ. According to most dictionaries, passion is a powerful often abandoned display of emotion such as love, joy, hatred, or anger. My personal definition is this: passion is a depth of love in which life becomes less important than the object of one's love or passion. Passion draws others towards its flame. Passion is contagious. Passion is at the heart of a proper emotional response to our God. Tap into this powerful emotion and see what happens to the songs you receive.

Song receiving means becoming a brush in the Creator Artist's hand.

As a Song Receiver, I try to do what I see Jesus doing in the Scripture. He painted pictures with words. I want to do that with song. Jesus painted word pictures with the parables. The Prodigal

75

son. Different kinds of Soils. Two foundations. Just read Matthew 7: 24-27. The sower. The tares and wheat. The mustard seed. Hidden treasure. A costly pearl. A net cast into the sea. See Matthew 13.

Pictures leave indelible impressions upon the canvass of our mind. Jesus knew that if He could get our minds to see the picture, we would not soon forget the Truth His words were trying to convey. Pictures help us draw upon the truth from the impressions left upon our minds.

As a brush in the hand of the Painter, we have at our disposal the use of literary 'devices' to help us paint unforgettable pictures. Those devices include allegory, metaphor, simile, and hyperbole. Following are brief definitions from The American Heritage Dictionary of each along with an example from some of my own songs.

Allegory

1.a. A literary, dramatic, or pictorial device in which characters and events stand for abstract ideas, principles, or forces, so that the literal sense has or suggests a parallel, deeper symbolic sense. b. A story, picture, or play in which this device is used. John Bunyan's Pilgrim's Progress and Herman Melville's Moby Dick are allegories.
2. A symbolic representation.
Examples:
•Sheep Song: Once upon a time two little lambs were lost...
•Daddy's Song

Metaphor

1. A figure of speech in which a word or phrase that ordinarily designates one thing is used to designate another, thus making an implicit comparison, as in "a sea of troubles"
2. One thing conceived as representing another; a symbol.
Examples:
•You are the River of Life...
•You are Light in the darkness...

Simile

A figure of speech in which two essentially unlike things are compared, often in a phrase introduced by like or as, as in "How like the winter hath my absence been" or "So are you to my thoughts as food to life" (Shakespeare).

Examples:
- Like a gentle stream, You're flowing...
- Like a glass, here is my heart...

Hyperbole

A figure of speech in which exaggeration is used for emphasis or effect, as in 'I could sleep for a year or This book weighs a ton.

Examples:
- A day in Thy courts is better than ten thousand outside...
- When I fell in love with You, You swept me off my feet...

What are the qualities of a good song?

Pure and simple, this is a very subjective question. What's good to one may not be good to another. My own view is that if a song works for me, it is good! That being said, there are qualities which I believe help make for a good song. We will discuss what I call the rules of good song writing and I will then discuss what the standard is in the 'real world' of Christian music.

From my perspective, a good song expresses my heart's deepest desires or concerns. A good song should stay with me as a reminder of Who God is and affirm me in my own identity as a new creation. A good song should be memorable and easy to sing. But 'easy' is a relative term. A song may not be good just because it is physically easy. Easy may mean it's easy for your soul to express your feelings back to Father God through a particular song. A good song leads me to a confrontation with God or simply to exalt and praise Him and consists of certain qualities like honesty, transparency, emotion, passion, and hope.

Honesty is a lack of deception. It evokes the genuine nature of our desire to be known by God and to know Him. Transparency is a state of the heart in which God can see through us because we have opened ourselves to Him...and others can see through us because we have nothing hidden. Emotion and passion are the rivers of communication from our being to the center of God's being. Hope is the always present reality that God is with us and has nothing but good on His mind concerning us.

What makes a song 'sing-able'? Music that is easily vocalized by people; a song that is 'user friendly.' A song that reinforces the truth of Who God is and who His worshipers are as a result. The characteristic of a song that draws the singer or player to express the musical qualities of that song from a deep emotional place in their heart and soul. It may be very difficult in a sense of execution, but easy because of the heart conveyed!

Rules of good song writing

Bottom line? I say, 'Hear God!' Touch His heart. In doing so, you will touch the heart of people as well. Standard song writing patterns or rules of the day say a good song will follow these 'rules':

    a. Popular pattern: verse-chorus-verse-chorus-bridge-chorus

    b. Memorable 'hook'

But again I say, if a song 'works,' forget the standard 'rules!'

Examples of songs that work in spite of the rules:

•When The Night Is Falling

•Lord, Though The World Rejected Me

•Nobody Fills My Heart Like Jesus

•You Are My All In All

Getting Started

What do I do to begin the journey of becoming a Song Receiver? Get ready by making preparations to receive. You cannot begin a journey unless you take that first step. Use simple, easy-to-use tools which are readily available. Always keep a Bible nearby (preferably several translations). Consider The Message and other modern translations. They tend to use very descriptive and creative ways of saying much-needed truth. You may wish to keep other literary tools available as well, like a Thesaurus, a Rhyming Dictionary, and a standard dictionary of some sort.

Do you have manuscript paper for melodic ideas? Get some. Do you have a notepad for lyrical ideas? Get one. How about a notebook for journaling? Do you have pencils and pens ready to write? Are you in a place where a piano or guitar is available? Even without these musical instruments, one can learn to hear with the heart and see with the mind well enough to hear and write down the songs God sings without ever going near an instrument.

Where is your digital voice recorder? Are your batteries fresh? Have you set aside time? Have you asked the Holy Spirit to fill you? Does Father know that like the psalmist, your tongue - your heart - is the pen of a ready writer? Get ready to receive. God is ready to sing. Be listening!

How do I get my songs heard?

I know. You have already received many songs that you believe would be beneficial to the body of Christ. Be patient and do not force yourself upon people. God's Word says, 'Do not exalt yourself in the king's presence, and do not claim a place among great men; it is better for him to say to you, "Come up here," than for him to humiliate you before a nobleman.' That is Proverbs 25:6-7 and it basically means don't force yourself upon people or you might just regret the humiliation later! Understand that your song may or may not be for the whole body. That's okay! For every song of mine that is in circulation, there are probably 20 more you will never hear!

Understand that even though your song may be for the whole body of Christ, the timing may not be now. Here's what I do. I use it in personal worship. I use it in small corporate and informal settings of worship. I make it available to my worship leader on both manuscript paper and on cassette tape or CD (mostly CD since I don't even have a cassette recorder anymore! You can make 'piano top' recordings and use them as ministry tools for others you are in relationship with.

Don't ever take 'rejection' of your song as an attack on your identity...or as personal rejection. Not every song is for everybody.

Share your songs with people you can trust. To share your children with someone who was going to put them down rather than build them up would be foolish. We are not to cast our pearls before swine. What do we do with pearls? We take them to people who will help us polish them and make them the best they can be!

Trust God to anoint your song. Anointing is really what we are after anyway. With God's anointing, great things can come from the most unlikely places. Also, trust Him to 'quicken' the hearts of people to their need for this song. Don't force it on anyone. But always remember - final judgment on anything you've written is yours - and yours alone!

CREATIVITY
...BUT IT'S NEVER BEEN DONE THAT WAY BEFORE...

Creativity

As I have already noted, creativity (to me) is seeing life and its circumstances from a different perspective. As a child of God Almighty, I must learn to see life from HIS perspective. To do so can prove to be one of the most productive means of unburdening your soul you may ever find in this life. To see tragedy from God's perspective gives hope. To view hurtful moments from God's point of view brings maturity and grace. To see your place and purpose from God's point of view brings passion and joy. To practice creativity in this manner is to be like our Father. He is Creator. We are made in His image. Let's learn to release more of our identity and be like Him. That is who we are. You get the picture. Following are some helpful tips to tapping into your identity as a creative being. They have helped me for years. May they do the same for you.

Refresh yourself

Sometimes, creativity means getting out of your regular routine. Have you considered taking a hike to help break the monotony of your job? Taking a hike may mean simply getting up and walking around the office. Such a walk may not seem too adventurous to you until you see that walk from God's perspective. Take time to look at the people around you from a different point of view. What are their needs? What are their dreams? What would bless them today?

Our souls need refreshment. What brings refreshment to you? Clearing the mind does wonders. Need help doing that? Call a friend who is always encouraging. Don't have any friends like that? Call someone who needs encouragement and YOU be that friend.

Take a praise break. Take just a few minutes and tell the Lord how much He means to you today. Get away from that computer or that knitting or that washing machine or that telephone for even 5 minutes and refocus on something that brings you joy...then apply that creativity to whatever creative outlet God has placed in your life.

Awaken your senses

Awakening the senses does not mean to do whatever feels good in a given moment. God gave us senses to help us understand the world and the people around us. Our senses were given with pure and holy intentions in mind. Creative people are often attacked in the area of erotic awareness of our senses. There is a place for that. Learn to use your senses in a godly manner. How can we learn to do this?

We must learn to see from God's perspective. When we see a loved one or a coworker, what do we see? What does God see? Learn to see with His eyes. When we hear someone speak, what do we hear? Do we listen beyond the surface and hear the meaning behind the sound, or are we too concerned with our own needs to hear from God's perspective? We know that children need to be touched. Have you ever been with someone you knew could benefit from your touch? A gentle touch on the arm that says 'I understand' or a pat on the back that says 'Way to go!' Have you ever wondered what an emotionally needy person might feel to go untouched in life? Learn to taste and see from God's perspective.

Color outside the lines

This is one of my favorite creativity boosters. I love it when people tell me things like 'you can't write a song that way. No one will ever sing it.' Telling me I can't do something is like pushing me off a cliff. What may look like a fall for someone else looks like an opportunity for adventure and creativity to me. I should walk around with a placard that says 'I'll show you!' Just because everyone does something one way doesn't mean it's the ONLY way. Maybe God has something else for you.

Laugh at yourself

I am convinced this is why I have children! Having open and honest relationship with my children guarantees I will hear whenever I act in a hypocritical way. The older I get, the more joy I find in learning to laugh at myself...especially when I think I have it all together. The Lord has amazing ways of reminding me that I'm the clay and He is the Potter! While driving down our country road with my children one day, one of my boys was talking with me about basketball. I was enthralled with the countryside around me. Just as Judah was commenting about a certain player in the NBA, I was making a comment about the mockingbird that flew across the road in front of me. I was in Steve Irwin (The Crocodile Hunter) mode, being the smart outdoorsman-expert-dad. Judah saw someone else. His take on the moment? "Dad, you're scaring me." Rather than become upset at how my children did not see the importance of my 'teaching moment,' I saw the utter hilarity from my son's perspective and began to laugh. I am too old to not enjoy my life. This joy can only serve to enhance my creative abilities and insights. Humility really is key in learning to laugh at one's self.

Go with what moves you

When I think about the things that inspire me to be creative in my gifting, I am always drawn toward inspiring stories. When I get down or distracted by the cares of my own life, I find it so useful to get my eyes directed somewhere else. My best creative times are when I focus on the Lord and His perspective...when I focus on meeting the needs of those around me...and when I focus on others who have overcome in some area of life. Reading about how Corrie Ten Boom survived and thrived through life in a Nazi prison camp birthed much power in my life to overcome and to be creative. The song There is No Chain was inspired by Corrie's story. When faced with the cost of leading others to freedom from homosexuality, I was greatly inspired by the life of William Wallace and the movie Braveheart. The song Love is Worth Living For came from this story. I enjoy talking with other overcomers. Whatever moves your heart, focus there for creative inspiration.

Create with others in mind

Hand in hand with what I just shared, I find that focusing on the needs of others - focusing on meeting the needs of others - inspires great and profound moments of creativity in my heart. As I write this, I have good friends who are facing death. The wife is in the last stages of her battle with cancer. The husband is watching his wife slip away. They told me of a dream that the Lord gave which has brought much comfort to their hearts. As I meditated on their circumstances and began to sing over them, the Lord gave a song based on the dream. It has brought much comfort to their last days together. Just last night, the husband called and told me how the Lord had used the song to minister to their grieving hearts...and he gave me permission to share the song publicly.

Of course, focusing on blessing God is always first in my mind. As my friend Kathy says, 'It's hard to doubt when you shout!' What she is really saying is that to shout to God in the midst of our circumstances is to refocus our minds on the only One is really in control! To focus on God is to focus on the very Giver of creativity - the Author and Creator Himself!

Explore your past

God's Word says in Isaiah 4:18-19, "Forget the former things; do not dwell on the past. See, I am doing a new thing! Now it springs up; do you not perceive it? I am making a way in the desert and streams in the wasteland." (NIV) We must learn to live our lives in such a way as to not allow our past failures to dictate future success, or in this case, future creativity. At the same time, one of my favorite passages of Scripture says, 'I remember my affliction and my wandering, the bitterness and the gall. I well remember them, and my soul is downcast within me. Yet this I call to mind and therefore I have hope: Because of the LORD's great love we are not consumed, for his compassions never fail. They are new every morning; great is your faithfulness.' (Lamentations3:19-23 NIV). We focus on our past as a means of remembering all God has done. This produces a grateful heart. Gratitude is a springboard into the deeper places of God's heart. In the deep places of God's heart there is a wealth of creative power. Remember the past. Don't live there. Allow God's hand in your life to produce gratitude. Be grateful for what you have, not what you don't have. Be grateful for what lies ahead. Don't fret over what you didn't accomplish in the past. Creativity waits for you in the place of gratitude.

Give yourself deadlines

We will dwell more on this subject in a later chapter, but it bears touching upon here. Procrastination is an enemy that debilitates our creative gifting. I find that I am more apt to carry out my plans if I give myself deadlines. I look ahead toward the goal I wish to reach and then begin to work out a plan backwards toward the start. I give myself small, achievable goals and set those goals on a timetable. I make realistic goals and tell others about them. This helps hold me accountable to keep working towards the goal. Having these parameters or boundaries gives me so much peace of mind that creativity generally begins to flow as soon as I can see the dates placed on the calendar pages. It's as if I can already see the accomplished goal. This gives me much hope. Proverbs 13:12 (NIV) says, *'Hope deferred makes the heart sick, but a longing fulfilled is a tree of life.'* Why put off hope? I always thrive when I have something to look forward to.

Be a risk-taker

For some people, taking risks is the essence of life. I have climbed mountains and have walked on ledges with 5,000 drops on either side. I have explored caves where I followed a string to find my way back out. I have jumped out of an airplane at 5,000 feet. I have gone SCUBA diving and swam with 12 reef sharks swimming around me for 45 minutes. I have skied the north face at Crested Butte and the double diamonds at Breckenridge. I have sung in front of 60,000 people. I have shared my story of redemption in honesty and battled the thoughts which are often the consequences of honesty. To take no risks is to close one's self off from life. If you risk nothing, you gain nothing. If you are afraid to risk loving someone else because you have been hurt in the past, you will not know love...because love requires relationship. Taking risks brings out the creativity God has placed in every living person. Jesus went to the cross knowing many would not see the purpose of His sacrifice or place their faith in Him. That must have hurt. That was the risk He was willing to take because He knew He needed to provide a way to relationship with God. His risk was life to me.

God's Word is clear concerning the need to be risk takers. Just read the parable of the talents in Matthew 25:14-30. God is seeking visionary men and women who are willing to take the risks required to see the Kingdom of God advanced. How do we overcome the fear of failure that often confronts us when risk is involved? We put on the truth. Truth leads to freedom. The first step toward truth always involves our honesty. The truth is, taking risks for the Kingdom of God will bless God and it will bless others. Failing to reach a goal or failing at a task does not equal failure. Just ask Thomas Edison if the 10,000 failed attempts at inventing the light bulb was worth the one success? Just ask Michael Jordan if all the missed baskets were worth the skill they helped build which exalted him to the highest ranks in NBA history. In each case, both would say they had not failed at those missed attempts. Edison would contend he hadn't failed. He had simply found 10,000 ways to not make a light bulb! Get God's perspective and be a risk taker - like Him.

Dream big

For years I heard people tell me my songs were too difficult for people to sing. My view was that people were more capable than we give them credit for. Many told me I could not succeed in the music business unless I was in Nashville. My view was that I wanted my family to not need a ministry like mine someday - so I would focus on them and Jesus and not worry about my ministry. Did this lessen my dreams? No way. I continued to dream big even though I chose to teach songs which were more complex than the popular worship choruses. What I found was that people were after deep, meaty music and lyrics which spoke to their deep needs. I continued to dream of making recordings that would reach places around the world. I continued to write music and write books even without a publisher because my dream said that others would need what I had to share. My dreams were often loftier than my human eyes could see a way to! DJ singing at the National Day of Prayer or ministering at the NCAA Final Four? Why not?!

I have learned that the Lord is the Dream Giver. If I can dream it, He can give the means to getting there! I write as if millions are going to sing my music. I write as if millions are going to be encouraged by the stories of God's grace and redemption ion my life. I not only set goals toward those dreams. I actually begin to walk toward my dreams! I act as if they are really going to happen - even if people think I am crazy! I dream outside the lines. One of my favorite motivators is for people to tell me something can not be done! Them's fightin' words to me! Dream big, then walk towards those dreams. God will begin to pour out creativity on your heart and life. As you come face to face with an obstacle to your dreams, God has a way of showing you a new perspective which takes you around, under, over, or right through those very obstacles!

Be open to adventure

Adventure can be simpler than an African safari. For most of us, adventure can mean getting to and from the grocery store without our brains being frazzled from the chaos and/or road rage that sometimes goes with it! Adventure can mean getting alone with your wife and dreaming together about the future. Adventure might mean flying a kite with your kids (or by yourself!). Adventure may mean ministering to someone else when you feel you need ministry yourself. Adventure is anything that takes our mind to a new place of joy and fulfillment that is out of the ordinary. What I have found through the years is that adventure, when seen from this perspective, actually becomes the norm. As with risk taking and dreaming, adventure puts us in the place where we need to hear from God. In adventure, we also often realize the effect of having our minds cleared as we focus on something which may be very out of the ordinary. Creativity flows in those moments where we need God or where we simply enjoy life with Him.

Imagine

Imagination is a gift from God. To use this gift, we must place ourselves in the midst of our dreams and goals. We must see ourselves at the end of our dreams even though we are not there yet! Do you desire victory in a certain area? Have you ever stopped to imagine what that would look like? Set goals according to these moments of imaginative creativity. One of the most powerful uses of imagination we have is to imagine what it would be like to be in God's very presence in heaven...to imagine what it would be like to stand and share my testimony before millions...to imagine or see myself as God sees me! Much creativity comes from using the gift of imagination.

Meditate

I have already touched on this subject, but it bears repeating because it has been one of the greatest tools in the palate of creativity God has given me. Practice taking just one word from Scripture and meditating on it all day. Go to bed asking the Holy Spirit to take you on a journey, delving into the meaning of that word. Ask Him to show you how it applies to your life or to the lives of those around you. As you go to sleep, ask the Spirit to meet you there in your dreams and to take you deeper into the meaning or concepts God wants you to derive from this word. Where the rubber meets the road is when you then take what you hear and apply it to your life and to the creative process.

Be disciplined

Plan creative time. Carve out even a few minutes every day. Follow your schedule...but be creative and flexible to the leadings of the Holy Spirit or to the needs of those around you. Don't be afraid to say 'no'. Others will fall in line to the way you do things - and they will learn to leave you alone. My own family knows that if I say I need to be alone that they are not to take it in a personal or hurtful way. They know Dad is hearing something from the Lord and by giving me some alone time they are actually helping and taking part in that process. We teach people how to treat us. We must learn that urgent does not equal important. A disciple is a follower. We must follow when He calls. Following a daily plan is one of the surest ways to get the creative juices flowing.

Fire your critics

I have enough people who are critical of my work. Heck, I'm more critical toward myself than I believe God wants me to be! He is God. I am not! That being said, I have learned not to cast my pearls before swine. What do we do with pearls - those jewels of great value - like ideas, or songs, or dreams? In the 'real' world, I would never place my pearls where a pig could trample on and ruin them. I would take my pearls to someone who could help me polish and refine them! I spend time with those who encourage and welcome my dreams and visions. I don't have time to waste on the dream killers. I don't have the right to be overly judgmental of myself. I, in fact, am commanded to love myself (Luke 10:27) so that I may more adequately love others around me! Spend time with other dreamers and encourage and polish their dreams and visions. Creativity is always the end result.

Surround yourself with life

Relationship requires giving and receiving. If I and my wife had never exchanged life by giving and receiving on a physical level, we would not have nine outrageously awesome children! Life is meant to be lived in relationship. To sequester ourselves away from others is to cut off our very life! Spend time encouraging friends. Spend time with your family. Share your creativity with others as a means of meeting their emotional, physical, or spiritual needs. Be a life giver. Surround yourself with life and watch the creativity come in floods you cannot even begin to keep up with!

Be a napkin writer

Creativity can come at the most inopportune times. I believe sometimes that God loves to watch me scramble around for something to write on. I have written songs on envelopes, magazine pages, napkins, and the back of my hand! No idea is a bad idea. Keep a folder of unfinished work and come back to it on a rainy day...or on a day when the inspiration isn't flowing so freely. See what God does...

Plan time to do nothing

Take time to clear your head by doing absolutely nothing at all.

Kathy, my manager, and I take time to schedule me time to do nothing. Some of my favorite mind-clearing, 'do-nothing' activities are getting my chainsaw out and heading to the woods, going fishing, wrestling with my boys, going to movies, like Napoleon Dynamite with my children, or giving myself permission to just sit and stare into space. Sabbath rest can come more easily if we learn to take time to do nothing. Creativity is always enhanced by this type of refreshment.

Reduce distractions

As with risk taking, my motto is "nothing ventured, nothing gained." What are your creative strongholds...those things that try to kill your creativity? If listening to the radio or watching TV take away or limit your creativity, then get rid of them or limit them. Name the strongholds or roadblocks in your creative life and deal with them. Use them for God's glory. If it's clutter, let it go. I periodically have my wife go through my stacks of stuff and throw away what I don't need. This helps clear the distractions those unfruitful piles can be. Learn to turn off other voices so you can hear more clearly. Finish tasks so they won't hinder/hamper your creativity. Unfinished tasks drain our minds as long as they are there staring at us. Don't be afraid to delegate. Creativity comes where the clutter is least.

Invest your life in others

This always leads to creativity. Inspiration is from God and should be used for godly purposes. Using our creative gifts to bless others is an endless well of creativity. I find more inspiration in this manner than in any other. I think this is God's heart. He is the God of relationship. Why did Jesus endure the cross? To restore us to relationship with Father God!

Listen for God's voice

Ask Him questions and then wait for the answer. Be expectant! Ask Him to speak to you through nature, through others, and through circumstances. Let Him know you are willing to hear/see through any means He might choose to speak.

Look outwardly

Depression comes very often from intense inner focus. When we focus our energies inwardly, and have no outward outlet, we lose touch with creativity. How do I overcome a lack of creativity and, in turn, get out of that inward focus on 'me?' I focus on God and worshiping Him. I focus on others and ministering to them. I set my eyes on the finish line of my life. I do not keep my eyes focused on my past. It exists, but it does not rule my present or further creative energies. If I am on a creative journey (which life is), I do not get to where I am going by focusing intently on the image in my rearview mirror. That would be crazy. I look toward the horizon and keep my eyes on the journey, only glancing briefly in the mirror to remember how far I've already come. Humility and brokenness are the keys to creativity and to right-focus.

Change your perspective

Although we have touched on this previously, here is yet another perspective on gaining another perspective! Be creative - create - in other mediums. If you are musical, paint or draw. If you dance, build a model airplane. If you sing, play an instrument. If you sculpt, go build a birdhouse out of wood. You get the point. Getting out of your box will help give you brand new points of view.

Don't be limited - Don't limit yourself

Who says you can't do anything you set your mind to? Psalm 24:1 says, "The earth is the LORD's, and everything in it, the world, and all who live in it." In other words, you belong to God. Everything in creation is made by His hand. He has given you a place in this world in which to create...and provided you with a wealth of resources by which to accomplish that creativity. Literally, the sky is the limit. Never let circumstances dictate your creativity.

Play with children

I have nine children...and nine new and unique points of view anytime I ask a question. One of the greatest joys of my life is simply playing with them. When they were little, I would help with the girls and their tea parties. The boys and I would wrestle (the girls, too!). I got down on their level and saw from their perspectives. I still do that. I play with my children and in the process learn a great deal about life. I learn to see life and situations as they do. Playing also brings joy. Joy brings laughter. Laughter is like a medicine for the soul. Be playful. Do you think God dreaded creating the earth? Or was He ecstatic and childlike in His glee? I think you know the answer. Be like Him who asked the disciples to bring the little children to Him.

Step away from your project

In creating a recording of my music, it is not uncommon to listen to a song literally dozens and dozens of times in the creative process. Sometimes, this leads to a numbness in my senses that leaves me without a gauge as to whether what I am hearing is in tune or not - the best performance or not. I have become too close to the project in those moments and need time away to refresh my senses. I take short breaks...a walk...lunch with a friend. And sometimes, I take several days off from the project. Rest your brain. Take time to cease from mental activity. Do something silly. Do things to help you laugh. Stepping away gives your creative resources and senses time to recharge.

Don't be in a hurry

Don't let your desire to finish diminish the excellence of what you are creating. I have waited for over two years to complete two major recording projects. Talk about impatient! I have had to learn to wait on the Lord. Sometimes He has more for me to say that needs to be added to the project. Sometimes I need to wait on the financial resources to complete a project. Sometimes, He just wants time with me. And time with Him equals creative inspiration.

Learn from others

I love to watch or read the biographies of others. I find so much inspiration in the stories of great men and women who have been overcomers in life. There is a wealth of untapped treasure in the life stories of great Christians. Another great resource of creative inspiration is in talking with people who inspire you! You usually have not because you ask not. If you want to meet and talk with a favorite artist, ask the Lord to make a way. And get ready to be filled with creativity in the process!

Show and tell

So many times God has given me a new song and it's been late at night...and I have called a couple of friends anyway! Even well after midnight! Sharing my creativity inspires more. So often, the response of someone I share a song with leads me to respond with another song! Share your creations with others. Use your creation as a blessing to others. While teaching my church's youth group about worship one summer, an entire album's songs were received! Those songs eventually became the recording Giant Killers because that is the name I gave this group of young people. Each week, the Lord would give me a new song to reinforce another truth. And the next week, the same thing would happen. On top of all this, the Lord used the music to help inspire a new devotional book based on my own life.

Capture your past

Writing your life story can lead to a host of forgotten inspiration in your own life. Years ago, I wrote my life story just as part of my own legacy to my children. In the process, much creativity was unleashed in my life. In writing my story, I was able to document all God has done in my life. Seeing God's hand in my life will serve to inspire others (like my children) to greater depths of faith. In the process, you will be greatly encouraged by just how much God loves you...regardless of your past!

Look around

Look around you...whatever environment you find yourself in. Look for God's hand in nature. See His handiwork in other people. Look for His artistic flare in the heavens. See His creative genius in the circumstances of your life.

Know your flow

Work when your creative juices flow the most freely. Utilize what works best for you, not what works best for others. I am a late night person. My wife is an early bird. We do not try to force ourselves to be creative in a way that actually works against our creativity. We give one another grace...and in the process a lot of creativity happens in our home.

Creative space

Have a special place - no matter how small - where you can keep your creative tools handy. Fill that space with things that inspire you. My daughter Galen keeps her oil paints in a huge plastic box she can take anywhere and set up as the mood requires. My daughter Glory has taken over a table in the barn where she has set up her torch for melting glass and creating exquisite beads. My wife Melinda has a rolling cart where she keeps all her jewelry making supplies. I have a small one room studio in a corner of my barn where I can hide away when necessary. The main creative space is between your ears. Set your mind at ease and you will have a constant creative space.

Celebrate the small things

You got the lawn mowed? Celebrate! An accomplishment is an accomplishment! Life is a creative journey, meant to be enjoyed! Take time to celebrate along the way. Share your joy with friends who appreciate your creativity. Share life with others.

Create with purpose

Knowing I have a purpose and a destiny inspires me to do great things. Knowing I am needed goes a long way in producing a creative atmosphere in my mind. I create to glorify God. I create to bless others. I create to let life flow from my heart as it was meant to be...it will help keep me healthy!

Get comfortable

When creating, wear something that makes you feel at ease. Some days I go to my studio in jeans and t-shirt. Some days I feel like dressing up and going to the studio. I dress to enhance my creativity. If I feel good about myself (or if I don't), dressing a certain way can help me get into a proper frame of mind. I also keep a small refrigerator stocked with Diet Coke in the barn. I have a plentiful supply of my favorite pens and pencils. The lighting in my studio is such that I can lower the lights as the mood necessitates. I make myself feel comfortable so as to enhance my creativity.

Stretch yourself

If we should not limit God in His creativity, why should we place certain limits on ourselves? Who says you can't achieve something God has placed in your heart to do? Dare to do the impossible. Who says you can't have a worldwide ministry in a rural Oklahoma town where you raise nine children with your wife and the worst traffic jam you face in the day is the 2 or 3 cars whose drivers wave at you as you pass on your lazy country lane? Huh?

Solitude

This has already been touched upon but bears saying one more time. Solitude restores the soul. Solitude: seclusion, isolation, privacy, retirement, retreat, hiding, concealment, reclusiveness, or withdrawal for a season is a spiritual act which leads us to deep intimacy with God. It is meant for sheer enjoyment of God's presence. Jesus practiced solitude from time to time. So should we. What solitude is not? Solitude is NOT loneliness: alienation, aloofness, detachment, desolateness, or isolation from God and others. Loneliness is caused by withdrawal due to hurt or rejection or fear which leads us away from the body which is a source of God's life and protection for us as believers - as creators.

HOW TO PLAN
A PROJECT
TO COMPLETION

STEP ONE...
STEP TWO...
STEP THREE...

How To Plan a Project to Completion

Whether recording an album or building a house, certain steps are required in order to see that project come to completion. I have met so many people who have big dreams - people who have undertaken great projects only to watch them fall apart or sit there gathering dust and cobwebs. Because they feel so overwhelmed by the weight of the still-unfinished task, the very daunting reality of the need to finish actually keeps them from finishing! In other words, if the enormity of a project gets bogged down by lack of finances, lack of help or support, lack of 'where-do-we-go-from-here? Wisdom,' it becomes easy to be overwhelmed and to give up. What I am sharing with you are simple tips I have learned the hard way in how to bring a project to completion.

1. Hear God

Because I am a believer, I begin the journey towards completion of a project by including the Lord in the process! Sounds simple, but how often do we include the Lord only as an afterthought...and generally only after we have made a huge mess and need Him to bail us out? More often than any of us would like to admit. So why not begin there? If we delight ourselves in the Lord, He will give us the desires of our heart (Psalm 37:4). What are your dreams and visions for the coming year? For the next five years? For today? By walking in intimacy with God, we come to delight in Him as He delights in us. When in an intimate relationship with the Creator, creativity is a natural byproduct. In His presence we see great dreams and visions for touching the world. Without dreams and vision, we wither up and die because we have nothing to look forward to. Know God and know your purpose. Know your purpose and you will dream. Once you have a clear understanding of just what you want to do and just where you need to go, ask God to show you what order of priority to give each dream or vision in terms of being individual projects. For me, that might mean I have two book ideas and three recording ideas I want to pursue. "Lord, which are front-burner ideas and which are back-burner ideas?" Once you know that, proceed to the next step.

2. Define each project

Once I have a sense of direction, I define each project. I give a full, written description of the project. This helps me clarify the magnitude and bring into focus many of the details needed to see it through. This helps me understand if the project is really needed or not. Will it meet the needs of people? What will be accomplished? How will it benefit others? How will it affect my family and my life? What are the various byproducts of this project? In other words, by creating the product, what 'spin-offs' will be required? Recording 'spin-offs' apart from CDs: songbook, Power Point lyric masters, accompaniment tracks, lead sheets/charts for band/orchestra, etc.

3. Count the cost

Once I have determined the full extent or scope of the project - at least to the ability I can see at the present time - I need to count the cost. This is a vitally important Scriptural principle that should be heeded when attempting any project. Jesus was being pursued by many people who wanted to be His disciples. He knew this would be a costly step for many, so He challenged them with these words:

"If anyone comes to me and does not hate his father and mother, his wife and children, his brothers and sisters — yes, even his own life — he cannot be my disciple. And anyone who does not carry his cross and follow me cannot be my disciple.

"Suppose one of you wants to build a tower. Will he not first sit down and estimate the cost to see if he has enough money to complete it? For if he lays the foundation and is not able to finish it, everyone who sees it will ridicule him, saying, -'This fellow began to build and was not able to finish.'

"Or suppose a king is about to go to war against another king. Will he not first sit down and consider whether he is able with ten thousand men to oppose the one coming against him with twenty thousand? If he is not able, he will send a delegation while the other is still a long way off and will ask for terms of peace. In the same way, any of you who does not give up everything he has cannot be my disciple." (Luke 14:26-33 NIV)

To blindly go into a project without facing the costs of that project is tantamount to suicide! It's crazy! Why set yourself up for failure? By counting the cost and planning properly, you virtually guarantee your very own success! It may take longer to bring your project to pass, but in the long run you learn many valuable life-lessons along the way which will only enhance the next project you are called upon to accomplish.

Counting the cost?

- Determine what each step will require in terms of time away from family or in terms of your relationship to God and to your employer.
- Determine what each step will require emotionally, mentally, and spiritually.
- Determine what each step along the way will cost in terms of time and money. Be realistic. What are you willing to sacrifice if your budget is small? Will this make a difference to you? Ask God to help you save the amount needed. Don't be afraid to work hard to see this project completed. God is Provider. If He does not provide, that could be a good indication of His will! (I personally do not plan a project unless I have the full amount needed to see it through. I have only varied from this practice once...and regretted it! I believe this is God's will for me. What you decide is God's will for you is between you and God!). The process of counting the cost is so important you should come back to it every so often along the way. After completing this step, you may wish to go to step 5 then come back and ask yourself these same questions. If your answers are acceptable to you, proceed! If not, continue to seek God.

4. Set a 'completed-by' date

My next step when approaching a project is to set a 'completed by' date. I ask the Lord to show me or give me a sense of when to have the final project ready for general release (as an album) or moving in (a building project). I then write that date on my calendar and then proceed to make a roadmap from where I am at present to where I will find the completed project. It's also like setting a date then working backward from the completion to where you are now.

5. Break the whole project into smaller goals or destinations

The overall project may seem overwhelming until you begin to see smaller, more readily achievable goals. Ask God to reveal all the necessary steps required to seeing your project completed. As with the overall project, assign a 'completed by' date to each step or goal and place each one on the calendar. Ask God to help you think creatively even in the planning process. Give Him the flexibility to show you shortcuts or new ways of doing things. Produce a detailed and concise 'road map' of the project from start to finish. Following is an example:

PROJECT XYZ   Completion date: April 1, 2006

Recording Completed by...	Step
	•Determine vision of project
December 1, 2005	
	•Select Producer
December 1, 2005	
	•Contract designer for cover
January 1, 2006	
	•Song selection
January 1, 2006	
	•Demo recorded
January 1, 2006	
	•Demo to all participants
January 5, 2006	
	•Marketing strategy/campaign
January 1, 2006	
	•Ministry opportunities
To be determined	

Recording Complted by...	Step *(continued from previous page)*
	•Mailing list
To be determined	
	•Arrangements Vocal/choral/BGV
February 1, 2006	
	•Band/orchestral
February 1, 2006	
	•Contract players/sessions •Book studio time
February 10-15, 2006	
	•Rhythm sessions
February 10-11, 2006	
	•Orchestral sessions
February 12, 2006	
	•BGV sessions
February 13,2006	
	•Solo Vocal/Instrumental sessions
February 14-15, 2006	
	•Select songbook producer
February 1, 2006	
	•Select other 'byproducts' producer
February 1, 2006	
	•Schedule mixing time
February 20-23, 2006	
	•Request other mixes: •Split Tracks •Tracks without lead instrument/vocal •Select reproduction contractor
March 1, 2006	
	•CDs/Songbooks/Etc. •Release of recording
April 1, 2006	

6. Delegate Responsibilities.

You cannot do this by yourself. Humility will go a long way in building up others along the way. When others are built up, they tend to feel needed! Assign different phases of the project to men and women you trust. After all, it's all about relationship. Work on building relationships and go out of your way not to burn any bridges. Any project ordained of God surely has a holy purpose...always to see others come to know Jesus and to bring Him glory...regardless of whether the project is 'religious' or 'secular'.

7. Get everything in writing.

Many good friendships have come to devastating ends because of simple misunderstandings. Contracts are not bad - even between family members! They simply serve as points of clarification and agreement between two fallible parties. This also provides accountability for the way you use your time and resources - God's children and His money! Contracts also help maintain the schedule you have established, even though a certain aspect of the project may be out of your direct control (CD duplication, printing, etc.)

8. Make yourself accountable to someone.

Entrust your heart and vision to those with whom you have a trust-based relationship. (Someone who will be honest with you, but will also allow you to be honest with them). Friends help us see when the way grows cloudy. A friendly shoulder comes in handy when needing a place to cry during times of loss or failure. Friends fill us with encouragement and give us strength to keep on keeping on when the way gets tough. Sharing our dreams and visions, our hurts and failures, our triumphs with another, is like multiplying our joy. Joy always begets joy. Put money (relationship) in this bank often and withdraw as needed!

9. Don't lose heart or grow weary

If, after great planning, the project is still not completed, reassess the project and begin looking for God's creative alternatives. Attempting great things for God is never in vain even if what we see appears to be a failure in earthly terms. Remember, Moses did not get to see the Promised Land, but without his part of the process, the children of Israel would never have gotten there. Remember, David did not get to see the completion of the temple, but his son, Solomon, did. Just because we don't get to see something completed in our lifetime does not mean we have missed God. We need to be able to creatively look at the Big Picture. To get that view we must learn to see from God's point of view. I guarantee, God is always up to something...and it is always with our best in mind. Dare to dream and remember Who gives those dreams is faithful in the midst of seeing them carried out.

> *"You lazy fool, look at an ant. Watch it closely; let it teach you a thing or two. Nobody has to tell it what to do. All summer it stores up food; at harvest it stockpiles provisions.*
> *So how long are you going to laze around doing nothing? How long before you get out of bed? A nap here, a nap there, a day off here, a day off there, sit back, take it easy-do you know what comes next? Just this: You can look forward to a dirt-poor life, poverty your permanent house guest!"*
> *Proverbs 6:6-11 (The Message)*

> *"Go to the ant, you sluggard; consider its ways and be wise! It has no commander, no overseer or ruler, yet it stores its provisions in summer and gathers its food at harvest. How long will you lie there, you sluggard? When will you get up from your sleep? A little sleep, a little slumber, a little folding of the hands to rest and poverty will come on you like a bandit and scarcity like an armed man."*
> *(Proverbs 6:6-11 NIV)*

HOW TO
ACHIEVE YOUR GOALS
ARE WE THERE YET?

How to Achieve Your Goals

When recording an album, much more goes into the process than meets the eye. People hear the finished product and think we went into the studio and came out a couple of days later without much thought of all that went into the whole 'ordeal' (and 'ordeal' is a good word sometimes in the recording process!). They don't see the heartache it often takes to receive the songs for a particular project...or the years of hard work and suffering we may have to endure to see it through. They don't see the many twists and turns we go through as we get into the process and realize we may not have heard God as clearly as we thought and have to change course in mid-stream. They don't see the hours and hours of arranging charts or the time spent in coordinating all the musicians and singers and studio time. They don't see the great financial or emotional cost that even the smallest of recordings can be. They don't see all the steps required to get a simple recording pressed into a form they can play in their stereo system. They don't see that, like the recording Giant Killers, the process has taken three years from the receiving of the songs to the final mix being made available to them in the form of a CD! If you could see all that is entailed, you would be tempted to give up sometime. So how do we see our goals through to completion?

First, I devote time to achieving my goals. If the goal is from God, then it is a priority for me...so I make time for it. I have learned to let God give me the desires of my heart by learning to delight in Him - and I'm not afraid or ashamed of receiving them! I practice giving the Lord the first-fruits of my visions by making the most of the time He has given me...for the days are evil. But at the same time, I am also quick to devote time to resting in Him and to resting physically. After all, what good is DJ if DJ gets burned out doing even good things?

As a dreamer, I cannot be afraid to change course along the way as God leads. I must allow God the freedom to redefine and revise my plans and dreams because He is the Potter and I am the clay. He sees clearly. I see through a glass, at best, very dimly. He is God. I am not! God does not change, but our perception and depth of maturity along the way will help us alter and refine our goals as we simply walk with and toward Him.

Remember, God is a God who risked everything by choosing to live His life through us. He gave us a free will and the choice to trust Him or reject Him...because love that is forced upon us is not love. So, I always remember I have choices along the way. How do I make those choices? I try to make decisions when my soul is at peace. If I don't have peace, I do not go. I have turned down many opportunities to travel around the world because I did not have peace. Hawaii. Taiwan. Israel. Call me crazy (and many have) but I must choose in the midst of peace. I choose, also, to believe God rather than my circumstances...and I remember that I do not have to do anything at all! But have learned that, like the ant continues to work and prepare for the winter that he knows is coming, I continue to work towards my goals even when it does not seem necessary...because I want to be ready when the time for completion is at hand! (Prov. 6:6-8). I try to live for today but know who holds the future. Like the virgins in Matthew 6:19-21, I must prepare wisely because I never know when the Lord will call for me to come and complete the goal. I believe the devil has a scheme but that God has a plan (thanks, Kathy!) so I plan to keep running the race even when I fall along the way (Micah 7:8). And here's a big one: I see failure as a teacher and not as a reason to give up! If the goal is from God and I fall, then I have an opportunity to see God display His creativity in and through me and my circumstances!

Above all, I see Christ as the ultimate goal I am trying to achieve. I seek Him in faith along the way (Heb. 11 :6). I want to know Him because to know Him is fulfillment and satisfaction (Phil. 3:8-11). To have a goal is to have a purpose. To have a purpose gives us a reason to live. To know Christ is the deepest desire of every human heart - whether they consciously know it or not! To seek that purpose brings fulfillment. The journey is where joy and anticipation are built, making the destination or fulfillment all the sweeter when we finally get there! We must lift Him up in all we do (Prov. 3:5-6) and remain focused by fixing our eyes upon the goal of knowing Jesus

(Heb. 12:2). And never ever give up or lose heart in our well-doing (Gal. 6:9) by - you guessed it - seeking to know Jesus!

I have learned that waiting on God does not mean doing nothing! We cannot wait for life to happen or it will pass us by. Who says we have to have a recording contract to record an album? Who says we have to live in Nashville to 'make it' in the music business? Who says I have to have a degree in Theory and Composition before 1 can write a song? Why do we listen to others when God's opinion may be the one we need to be paying attention to? You can have all the visions in the world but see none of them come to pass if you do nothing about them! You will reap what you sow. Sow the visions of your heart on the soil of your resources and abilities and then trust the Water of the Word to quench your thirst and the Bread of Life to bring forth nourishment along the way...and you will see fruit as the Spirit fills your life with the very vision and creativity and breath of God (Gal. 5:22).

Again, what do I do if my dreams or visions don't pan out? We must remember where dreams come from in the first place (Psalm 27). They are from God! If we see death, we must learn to ask God to bring life from death we experience. And remember, the death of Jesus did not deter the Father's vision of redemption for mankind because our God is a God of resurrection! It is perfectly acceptable to ask the tough question of whether our dreams or visions are really from God (Ps. 37:4). We won't know until we ask! And if they are not, we get to go on to something new and wonderful from our Father! God may be trying to bring greater clarity and simplicity to your dream. God is more creative than we! Perhaps you are only a small part in seeing the fulfillment of your dream. He may bring it to pass through one of your children or through some other means you haven't even thought of. Moses had the dream for the Promised Land, but the fulfillment came through another. Remember also that when a vessel is broken, the fragrance of life can pour through more freely. How you and I respond to death of a dream or vision determines whether life will be accomplished - or death. In such times, we must quickly draw near to Father God in quietness and confidence because He is the Dream Giver and the Dream Maker.

And do not ever stop dreaming unless He says to!

In putting down the giants that try to hinder achieving my goals, I have learned the value of spending time with other dreamers. I do not cast my pearls (dreams) before swine (those who would trample on them) but I share them with those who will help me polish them! Relationship is vital for life to take place. Fellowship with others in the body. We really do need one another to see our visions and goals come to pass. It is always good to have others watching our perimeters because they help us see the lies and pitfalls and giants a little more clearly and we can respond with much more grace and wisdom.

God is a big God...so dream big! Dreams can be very simple or very complex. In dreaming and achieving goals, it is vital that we always remember who and whose we are. What is seen on the outside by others should merely be a reflection of what is taking place on the inside of our hearts. We always have a choice in how we respond to life...and life is better enjoyed by dreaming and heading toward the goal set before us... that of knowing Christ on an intimate level.

Some of my dreams and goals that have helped shape my life along the way? The goal of having my life and mind so transformed that what was once homosexual is now heterosexual. Where I was overcome with bitterness for all those who had used me along the way is now love and forgiveness. I had the goal of seeing my despair turned to joy. Impatience to patience. Harshness to gentleness. Anger to peace. Jealous heart to encouraging heart. Worry to trust. Out of control, to self-control. Recording. Writing. Husband. Father. Inventor. Minister. Dreamer. Visionary. So many goals...and eternity to see them come to pass!

Question for meditation:
• What are the goals of your immediate life?
•What is God's perspective for those goals?
•Have you heard God clearly?
•What should you do if you are not sure?
•What do you plan to do if God directs you to change course in midstream?

•What dreams have you lain down as unachievable that perhaps you should pick back up?

•Have you limited God in any way concerning your dreams?

A FINAL WORD

KNOW GOD...
    KNOW YOURSELF...
KNOW OTHERS...

A Final Word

Some people have been anointed to lead worship in huge churches where the budgets are seemingly endless and thousands attend each service. Some are anointed to lead worship for the homeless. Which is more important? Some are anointed with great financial and physical resources. Some live from paycheck to paycheck and must be creative with little. Which is most important? Still others are anointed to write songs which sell millions of copies while others are anointed to write songs heard only by a few dozen and the hosts of heaven? Which is more needed? In whatever state you find yourself, the answer is the same. We are to love God and love others as we love ourselves.

Whether we are musicians or not...whether we are pastors or Sunday School teachers or not...whether we work a white collar or blue collar job...if we are new creations in Christ - God's children - we are called to minister. Because we are His children and are created in His image, we are made to be creative...like our Father. To be all God has called us to be, we must remember a few basic truths in order to fully capitalize on the unique way He has made us as individuals. Regardless of our gifts, talents, social status, career choice, gender, or age, we would do well to learn to walk in intimate relationship with God and to live our lives according to a very basic principle of love and worship found in Luke 10:27...

> *"Love the Lord your God with all your heart and with all your soul and with all your strength and with all your mind'; and, 'Love your neighbor as yourself."*

In order to love God...to love ourselves...to love others, we must:

1. Know who God is and acknowledge Him relationally in our lives.

Knowing Him is worth any struggle I must endure in this life. Knowing Him intimately requires all of our being directed toward

112

Him...and understanding that all His being is directed toward us! Amazing. With all we are, we are to worship Him.

> ...whatever was to my profit I now consider loss for the sake of Christ. What is more, I consider everything a loss compared to the surpassing greatness of knowing Christ Jesus my Lord, for whose sake I have lost all things. I consider them rubbish, that I may gain Christ and be found in him, not having a righteousness of my own that comes from the law, but that which is through faith in Christ — the righteousness that comes from God and is by faith. I want to know Christ and the power of his resurrection and the fellowship of sharing in his sufferings, becoming like him in his death, and so, somehow, to attain to the resurrection from the dead.   Philippians 3:7-11 (NIV)

2. Know who you are in Christ.

I am who my Father says I am. Temptations, feelings, past failures, worldly wisdom - none of these define me. I belong to Him. One cannot properly love his neighbor if he has not accepted his position in Christ. We behave out of who we believe we are. Once, I believed I was homosexual. I do not believe that is who I am anymore by virtue of the cleansing work of the blood of Jesus. And guess what? I act like one who is free! If I can believe this for and about myself, guess what? I will treat others the way God would because I have learned to see beyond the flaws and see the child God wants as His own...and love them as Christ loved me! With all we are, we are to be who He has called us to be.

> Therefore, if anyone is in Christ, he is a new creation; the old has gone, the new has come! 2 Cor. 5:17 (NIV)

> Neither circumcision nor uncircumcision means

113

anything; what counts is a new creation. Gal. 6:15 (NIV)

3. Love your neighbor.

Who is your neighbor? Whomever you happen to be with in any given moment! Jesus spent time with the rejected ones in his society. Jesus came for the lost and abandoned of the world. He came to rescue the perishing, wounded sheep. We are called to do the same. If we are more consumed with 'making it' in the music business than we for the people whom Christ gave His life for, we are nothing more than a noisy, clanging gong. With all we are, we are to go after the lost sheep.

> *Even so it is not the will of your Father which is in heaven, that one of these little ones should perish.*
> *Matthew 18:14 (KJV)*

> *For the Son of Man came to seek and to save what was lost.* *Luke 19:10 (NIV)*

> *All this is from God, who reconciled us to himself through Christ and gave us the ministry of reconciliation...* *2 Cor. 5:18*

> *Greater love hath no man than this, that a man lay down his life for his friends.* *John 15:13*

A man wishing to make himself appear holy by his works Once asked Jesus a question:

> *...he wanted to justify himself, so he asked Jesus, "And who is my neighbor?" In reply Jesus said: "A man was going down from Jerusalem to Jericho, when he fell into the hands of robbers. They stripped him of his clothes, beat him and went away, leaving him half dead. A priest happened to be going down*

114

*the same road, and when he saw the man, he passed
by on the other side. So too, a Levite, when he came
to the place and saw him, passed by on the other side.
But a Samaritan, as he traveled, came where the man
was; and when he saw him, he took pity on him. He
went to him and bandaged his wounds, pouring on
oil and wine. Then he put the man on his own donkey,
took him to an inn and took care of him. The next
day he took out two silver coins and gave them to
the innkeeper. 'Look after him,' he said, 'and when
I return, I will reimburse you for any extra expense
you may have.'*

*"Which of these three do you think was a neighbor to
the man who fell into the hands of robbers?"*

*The expert in the law replied, "The one who had
mercy on him."*

Jesus told him, "Go and do likewise."
Luke 10:29-37 (NIV)

Life and ministry really are simple if you choose to see them from God's perspective. It's all about Him and His glory. Take your gifts and talents, dreams and situations, and love your God. Take your unique abilities and visions and love yourself by walking in the identity He has given you. Take all God has given you and give Him thanks by laying down your life for others...just as He laid down His life for you. In so doing, you will tap into wells of creativity, song receiving, and ministry you never dreamed possible in this life. Go and be His song to a hurting world.

Other books and CDs by Dennis Jernigan -

Books:

Giant Killer
> a book for those who desire freedom from bondage -
> Dennis Jernigan's personal story of how he came to know
> freedom from homosexuality

Help Me to Remember
> a book for those who grieve or for those who desire to
> minister to those who grieve

This is My Destiny
> a study of our identity in Christ

A Mystery of Majesty
> a study of the great majesty of God

CDs:

I Surrender
This is My Destiny
Giant Killers
Hands Lifted High - a collection of Dennis Jernigan singing his music with many of today's top Christian recording artists such as Natalie Grant, Twila Paris, Ron Kenoly, Charlie Hall, Rebecca St. James, Annie Herring, Matthew Ward, Russ Taff, Watermark, Charmaine, Jeff Deyo, Alvin Slaughter, Russ Taff, and Travis Cottrell

Dennis has recorded more than 25 albums of original music. For more information:

Shepherd's Heart Music, Inc. - 1-800-877-0406
3201 N. 74th St. West
Muskogee, Oklahoma 74401

www.dennisjernigan.com

Printed in the United States
51967LVS00002B/34